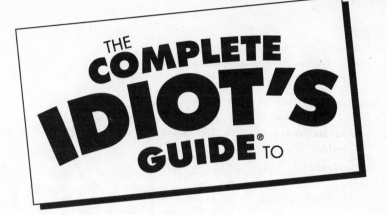

THE COMPLETE IDIOT'S GUIDE® TO

Sensational Salads

by Leslie Bilderback, CMB

ALPHA

A member of Penguin Group (USA) Inc.

ALPHA BOOKS

Published by the Penguin Group

Penguin Group (USA) Inc., 375 Hudson Street, New York, New York 10014, USA

Penguin Group (Canada), 90 Eglinton Avenue East, Suite 700, Toronto, Ontario M4P 2Y3, Canada (a division of Pearson Penguin Canada Inc.)

Penguin Books Ltd., 80 Strand, London WC2R 0RL, England

Penguin Ireland, 25 St. Stephen's Green, Dublin 2, Ireland (a division of Penguin Books Ltd.)

Penguin Group (Australia), 250 Camberwell Road, Camberwell, Victoria 3124, Australia (a division of Pearson Australia Group Pty. Ltd.)

Penguin Books India Pvt. Ltd., 11 Community Centre, Panchsheel Park, New Delhi—110 017, India

Penguin Group (NZ), 67 Apollo Drive, Rosedale, North Shore, Auckland 1311, New Zealand (a division of Pearson New Zealand Ltd.)

Penguin Books (South Africa) (Pty.) Ltd., 24 Sturdee Avenue, Rosebank, Johannesburg 2196, South Africa

Penguin Books Ltd., Registered Offices: 80 Strand, London WC2R 0RL, England

000310

Copyright © 2009 by Leslie Bilderback, CMB

International Standard Book Number: 978-1-59257-825-2
Library of Congress Catalog Card Number: 2008935065

11 10 09   8 7 6 5 4 3 2 1

Interpretation of the printing code: The rightmost number of the first series of numbers is the year of the book's printing; the rightmost number of the second series of numbers is the number of the book's printing. For example, a printing code of 09-1 shows that the first printing occurred in 2009.

Printed in the United States of America

Note: This publication contains the opinions and ideas of its author. It is intended to provide helpful and informative material on the subject matter covered. It is sold with the understanding that the author and publisher are not engaged in rendering professional services in the book. If the reader requires personal assistance or advice, a competent professional should be consulted.

The author and publisher specifically disclaim any responsibility for any liability, loss, or risk, personal or otherwise, which is incurred as a consequence, directly or indirectly, of the use and application of any of the contents of this book.

Most Alpha books are available at special quantity discounts for bulk purchases for sales promotions, premiums, fund-raising, or educational use. Special books, or book excerpts, can also be created to fit specific needs.

For details, write: Special Markets, Alpha Books, 375 Hudson Street, New York, NY 10014.

Publisher: *Marie Butler-Knight*
Editorial Director: *Mike Sanders*
Senior Managing Editor: *Billy Fields*
Senior Acquisitions Editor: *Paul Dinas*
Senior Production Editor: *Megan Douglass*
Copy Editor: *Jan Zoya*

Cover Designer: *Becky Harmon*
Book Designer: *Trina Wurst*
Indexer: *Angie Bess*
Layout: *Ayanna Lacey*
Proofreader: *Mary Hunt*

Contents at a Glance

Contents

Introduction

Soup or salad? Salad, of course!

Fresh, crunchy, delicious, and good for you, salads are one of the most popular dishes in American cuisine. Every menu has them; every well-balanced meal includes them; and now you can create a treasure trove of delicious, classic, and unique salads for your family and friends.

The idea that fresh greens and vegetables are healthful is not a new one. People as far back as the ancient Egyptians, Romans, and Greeks enjoyed salads of greens and vegetables. They dressed them with oil, vinegar, and salt and called them *salata*, meaning "salted things."

Vegetables were enjoyed in this manner until the late 1800s, when the science of home-making became popular. In that day and age, neater and cleaner meant better and more refined. In such a home, no messy pile of raw leaves would do. Obsessed with hygiene, cooks figured the best way to avoid sickness was to cook the germs out of their veggies (along with flavor and nutrients). To accommodate the loss of flavor, ingredients of all kinds were added, mixed, and molded. Salads were deconstructed, organized, and arranged—and bore little resemblance to the food they were made from.

At the turn of the twentieth century, salad dressings began to appear on the market. New York deli owner Richard Hellman sold his mayonnaise to the public in the 1920s, and Kraft introduced pourable French dressing in 1925. In 1948, Phil Sollomi, owner of the Wishbone restaurant in Kansas City, Missouri, began selling his mother's Spicy Sicilian salad dressing.

Several Midwestern restaurants claim to have invented the salad bar in the 1960s. This development made fresh salads possible in a fast-food setting and many full-service restaurants adopted the trend as a way to keep their customers busy while the "real" food was being cooked. Today, nearly every restaurant offers at least a small selection of salads, and most provide salads as full-blown entrée choices. With a virtually unlimited supply of fresh greens, vegetables, and fruits from around the world, salad-making has risen to new heights in the hierarchy of food.

Granted, most salads are not "health food." The healthy myth stems from the use of vegetables. Sure, vegetables are good for you, but many salads are also loaded down with caloric dressing, croutons, fruits, nuts, meats, and cheese. All that can be as dangerous to your waistline as a double cheeseburger. If you're concerned with your youthful figure, eat salads as a part of a well-portioned, well-balanced diet. But the vegetable component is an important one, and it is necessary to note that few Americans get their recommended 3 cups a day. So drowned in dressing or not, the nutrients derived from fresh vegetables are infinitely better for you than popping a daily multivitamin.

When shopping for produce, look for the dark, vibrant colors, which is an indication of the nutrients within. The darker the hue, the more nutrient-packed it is.

And remember that it's important to keep variety on your menu. Having the same foods every day limits the amount of nutrients you get. A healthier diet is an ever-changing diet. But getting stuck in a culinary rut is easy to do, and coming up with new recipes can be challenging. There's no loss for salad inspiration within these pages. Soon you'll be wowing your family and friends with tantalizing salads every day of the week. So dust off your salad spinner, head to the market, and chill your plates. It's salad time!

How to Use This Book

This book is dedicated to providing you with a number of delicious, easy-to-prepare, nutrient-rich salad recipes. What's more, it's a font of creative ideas you can use to create your own salad sensations.

In **Part 1, "Salad Basics,"** you get to know produce like never before. These chapters discuss how to pick it, store it, and the best methods of preparation. Vegetables, fruits, oils, and vinegars are all covered, as well as some nifty techniques for creating your own flavored oils and vinegars.

Salads traditionally served as side dishes comprise **Part 2, "Salads on the Side."** Here you'll find greens salads, potato salads, fruit salads, and even warm salads—all suitable to accompany your favorite meal, whether its filet mignon or PB&J.

Part 3, "The Main Event," investigates the salad as an entrée. Filled with meat, poultry, seafood, pasta, grains, and beans, these salads are designed to fill you up, physically and nutritionally. There's even a chapter for salads whose ingredients are taken from some of your favorite main courses, such as tacos, BLTs, fajitas, and Chinese chicken.

Accoutrements

Throughout the book you'll find a sprinkling of sidebars to complement the text:

 Heads-Up!
These boxes issue warnings for common mistakes and potential disasters.

 Lettuce Lingo
Look here for culinary terms you might not know.

 Salad Secret
These boxes contain tips and tricks every good cook should know.

 Tasty Morsel
These boxes are full of interesting facts you never knew you needed to know.

Acknowledgments

This book is dedicated to Bill, who, once upon a time, made the most romantic dinner ever. He spent all day shopping, washing, and chopping to create our very own salad bar. Love at first bite! Thanks to that salad bar, we now have two more salad lovers, Emma and Claire. Girls, why not try something besides blue cheese?

Special Thanks to the Technical Reviewer

The Complete Idiot's Guide to Sensational Salads was reviewed by an expert who double-checked the accuracy of what you'll learn here, to help us ensure that this book gives you everything you need to know about turning out terrific salads at home. Special thanks are extended to Lisa Vislocky.

The Complete Idiot's Guide to Sensational Salads

Trademarks

All terms mentioned in this book that are known to be or are suspected of being trademarks or service marks have been appropriately capitalized. Alpha Books and Penguin Group (USA) Inc. cannot attest to the accuracy of this information. Use of a term in this book should not be regarded as affecting the validity of any trademark or service mark.

Part 1

Salad Basics

Is your idea of salad a bowl of lettuce and a bottle of dressing? Do you get nervous in the produce section of your grocery store? Are you aching for more in your salad relationships? If so, you've come to the right place.

Any ingredient that could conceivably be used in a salad is explained in the following two chapters. You learn about the different greens, herbs, vegetables, fruits, and extras that make salads interesting and fun. Then, you learn how to put down the bottle and make your own delicious dressings from scratch. Creamy and thick, tangy and light, and everything in between, these basic recipes cover it all.

Chapter 1

More Than Just Lettuce

In This Chapter

- ◆ Graceful greens
- ◆ The skinny on vegetables
- ◆ Fruits 101
- ◆ Tools of the salad-making trade

The number of salads you can create is infinite. After all, you can toss together nearly any ingredients and call it a salad. In fact, that's precisely how a lot of our favorite salads came into being. The Cobb salad, for instance, was nothing more than an artful use of leftovers. Fruit salad was a clever way to create a healthier dessert. And tuna salad was a desperate attempt to get folks to use tuna fish, an unpopular ingredient newly available in cans in the 1950s.

Despite the salad's humble pedigree, wonderfully flavorful and enticing dishes can be created and shared in salad form. The key to success is in the ingredients. Fresh greens, vegetables, and fruits—bought, cleaned, and stored with care—can make an ordinary salad fabulous.

Great Greens

When you think about salad, the typical green salad probably springs to mind. The *green* refers to lettuce, and although you have your pick of dozens of lettuces, most salad bowls contain iceberg. Pale, bland, and devoid of much nutritional value, *iceberg lettuce* is synonymous with *salad* to most Americans. But iceberg lettuce has the least nutrition of any lettuce, and although the standard house salad made from chopped iceberg and bottled Ranch dressing has its place, far more interesting creations are just waiting for you. So why not mix it up a little?

Make It Colorful

Let's start with color. Color is an indication of the vitamins found within a plant. Generally, the more nutrients a plant has, the darker its color is.

Green leafy vegetables are a major source of iron, antioxidants, vitamin C, beta-carotene, calcium, and folic acid. They are also low in calories—1 cup has about 100 calories. Each leaf also contains an enormous amount of vital fiber, and greens act as a natural breath freshener, too.

Tasty Morsel

The pigment that gives green leafy vegetables their color is chlorophyll. Chlorophyll is beneficial in helping prevent and treat certain cancers.

Coincidentally, color is also an indication of flavor. If there's color in the leaf, you can be assured it also has a vivid flavor. So go dark whenever possible.

Washing Greens

Most lettuces grow in sandy soil and need a thorough washing before being added to the salad bowl. But lettuces are delicate, leaves bruise easily, and those precious greens can go bad quickly if not stored properly.

The best way to wash greens is to submerge them in cold water. Fill a sink or large container with cold water. Pull the leaves off the heads if possible, and soak them for a couple minutes, swishing them gently in the water. Pull them out of the water, leaving the dirt and sand to sink to the bottom. Drain the sink and repeat one or two more times as necessary. Dry the greens in a salad spinner, or let them air dry in a colander before patting them dry with paper towels. Wet greens will water down the salad dressing and cause the leaves to spoil more quickly.

If you don't plan on using your greens right away, store them cleaned, layered between pieces of paper or linen towel, packed airtight in a plastic tub or zipper bag, in your refrigerator's crisper. This keeps them crisp and prevents wilting, and the towel soaks up excess water that can cause spoilage.

> **Heads-Up!**
>
> Many salad greens are available prewashed and trimmed and ready to pour into the salad bowl. This is super-convenient, but beware: after the bag is opened, these lettuces deteriorate much more quickly than lettuce still attached to a head.

Greens A to Z

Now let's look at some of the delicious, nutritious greens you can use to create your salad:

Arugula   A member of the chicory family, also known as roquette or rocket, arugula has a peppery flavor that intensifies with age. It holds up to stronger flavors like nut oils, strong vinegars, and pungent cheeses. The narrow, slightly pointed leaves last for several days in the refrigerator if they're first wrapped in a damp towel.

Belgian endive   Often referred to simply as endive, the pale white leaves of this small, tightly compacted, pointed head are grown using a method called blanching. Covered in soil as it grows, the plant is denied light to prevent the development of chlorophyll, which would make it bitter. Look for yellow leaf tips because the greener they get, the more bitter the leaf. Belgian endive is also known by its Dutch name, *witlof,* or "white leaf."

Butterhead   Also known as Boston or Bibb lettuce, this leaf is identified by the shape of its head, which opens loosely, like a rose. The flavor is very mild, and the texture, especially that of the heart, is soft and "buttery." Its leaves wilt quickly, so wash it at the last minute before serving.

Chicory *Chicory* is a pseudonym for several lettuces, but it's actually the name of an entire genus that includes several types of endive, radicchio, and escarole.

Cress *Cress* refers to several members of the cabbage family eaten as green vegetables and herbs. Watercress is the most common. Although it's mostly seen as a garnish (or as the filling for a tea sandwich), cress's peppery crunch makes it an interesting addition to salads. Other species include garden cress, land cress, and winter cress.

Dandelion This is the very same plant you're fighting with on your lawn. You can also enjoy its tender, pleasantly bitter, mustardy-flavored greens. They are high in vitamins A and C and calcium and have more iron than spinach. Pick them while they're young and tender, before the weed-whacker gets 'em.

Heads-Up!

Most greens start their lives sweet or mild in flavor and grow increasingly bitter as they age. Keep that in mind when choosing your leaves.

Escarole Another member of the chicory family, escarole has wide, wavy leaves and a yellow-white heart that can be somewhat bitter, although less so than curly endive. Its bitterness can be balanced nicely with sugar and salt. Try it with a simple vinaigrette made with a touch of honey.

Frisée This salad green, sometimes called curly endive or simply chicory, has wild, frizzy, green-edged leaves. It has a slightly bitter, crisp taste and a crunchy texture. The inner leaves are milder. Avoid leaves that have turned yellow.

Iceberg This lettuce has relatively little in the way of nutrition, but it does supply a hearty crunch and good amount of water, which is refreshing on a hot summer night. Look for tight, firm heads. It browns quickly after it's cut, so peel off only the leaves you need and store the rest in your crisper.

Mache Also known as lamb's lettuce or corn salad, this leaf is dark green and velvety, providing an interesting texture that stands out among other ingredients. It grows in tiny bunches of rounded leaves that are very fragile and bruise easily. The flavor is mild and appropriate with a variety of vegetables, fruits, meats, and spices.

Mesclun   *Mesclun* means "mixed," and it was traditionally a mix of wild shoots and leaves that sprouted up in the spring. Today mesclun is cultivated and is available at most supermarkets, usually under the name "spring mix." The mix often includes dandelion, arugula, cress, chervil, and a variety of mild lettuces, like curly green or oak leaf.

Oak leaf   Named for the shape of its leaf, this lettuce is related to the butterhead and has a similarly mild flavor. Leaves are curly and red and grow in a loose head. There's also a green variety.

Radicchio   Another lettuce from the chicory family, radicchio is best known by its maroon leaves with white veins. It has a slightly bitter, slightly spicy flavor, which mellows when heated. The most common variety has a head about the size of a grapefruit. Radicchio is sometimes known as Italian chicory; also look for *radicchio di Treviso*, which is similar in appearance to its cousin Belgian endive although slightly larger and purple.

Romaine   Also known as cos, romaine has large, sturdy leaves with one big, crunchy vein, or rib, running down the center. This widely available lettuce is the traditional leaf used in Caesar salad.

Spinach   Spinach is a nutritional powerhouse, in vitamins A, C, E, and K; magnesium; iron; calcium; and antioxidants. Its leaves sprout in small bunches from sandy soil and should be washed thoroughly several times before using. You can eat the young stems, but be sure to remove larger stems because they're fibrous and bitter.

Tasty Morsel

Spinach does not have an unusual amount of iron; it's comparable to most other green vegetables. Perhaps Popeye helped perpetuate the iron myth. Or it could have been the doctor in the late 1800s who published the iron content with the decimal in the wrong place.

Versatile Vegetables

Any vegetables can be made into a salad, and although they're all good for you, they're obviously not all the same. Roots, shoots, beans, and peppers all have their own distinctive traits and must be treated with respect if you want to bring out their best qualities.

To make cooking easier, wash veggies when they come home from the market. Store them clean, wrapped in plastic, in your refrigerator's crisper or in a bowl in a cool, shadowy spot on your counter.

The Dirt on Root Vegetables

By definition, root vegetables grow in the dirt. Potatoes, beets, carrots, parsnips, celery roots, and radishes typically get a cursory rinsing prior to hitting your market, but a thorough scrub at home is usually a good idea. Store washed roots in the crisper, and remove any attached greens because they spoil quickly.

You can cook root vegetables a couple ways. Boiling is fast and easy: cover with cold water, bring to a boil, reduce heat to a simmer, and cook until tender. A fork inserted into the cooked veggie should slide in and out easily. But be aware that boiling removes a fair amount of nutrients and pigments, and the vegetable itself absorbs water. After boiling, as it sits, the vegetable loses some of this absorbed water, which could dilute the recipe.

Roasting is a more flavorful method of cooking roots. The all-around heat evaporates their water, concentrating the flavors within, and caramelizes the outer surface. Cut roots into 1- or 2-inch cubes, toss in a light coating of oil (whatever your recipe recommends), sprinkle with salt, and spread onto a baking sheet in one even layer. Be sure to get them in a single layer, because a mound of vegetables won't cook evenly.

 Heads-Up!

When roasting or boiling, be sure all the pieces are cut in a uniform shape and size. Smaller pieces cook faster than big ones, and if they're mixed, the small ones will be overdone before the big ones are ready.

Roots can also be grated or sliced and fried. Be careful not to grate or slice the roots too far in advance of cooking, though, because they'll dry out quickly, and some, like potatoes and celery roots, will oxidize, or turn brown. The color doesn't hurt you, but it sure isn't appetizing.

Tender Shoots, Beans, and Peas

Several different vegetables are young, tender, and green and can all be prepared in the same way, with minimal heat. Among them are asparagus, broccoli, green beans, peas, and summer squash. These veggies are often interchangeable in recipes because, although their flavors are different, they share a color and texture.

Like all vegetables, these are packed with vitamins and minerals and offer the most health benefits when they're eaten raw. Cooking them yields a more tender product, but overcooking leaches out all the color, flavor, and nutrients. Overcooking happens fast with these vegetables, so pay close attention to produce the best product. The key is in the color.

This cooking process has several names, include blanching, par boiling, and al dente. It involves dropping the vegetable into boiling water for under a minute, until the color brightens and the texture softens slightly. Then they're removed and immediately dropped into ice water to stop the cooking process.

All these vegetables should be stored in air-tight containers in the refrigerator, where they'll keep for about 5 days.

Vegetables A to Z

Now that you know what lettuces or greens you're starting your salad with, it's time to add the veggies!

Artichokes Artichokes are probably most familiar served steamed or boiled, with the leaves ripped off and dipped in butter, mayo, or garlic aioli. Those leaves, which are often lovingly gnawed clean of choke, can be trimmed away to reveal the tender heart, which makes a fantastic addition to any salad. After peeling off loose leaves, use a sharp knife and pare away the darkest leaves, down to the yellow-green tender leaves and heart. Scoop away the choke, the purple inner thistle, with a spoon. Submerge pared artichokes in acidulated water to prevent browning.

Asparagus Asparagus is actually the young shoot of a fern in the lily family. It has been enjoyed as a vegetable and used medicinally since biblical times. White asparagus is grown by a process called blanching, in which shoots are covered with dirt to prevent the formation of chlorophyll. Choose firm, small shoots when possible, and simply trim off the cut end. You can peel thicker stems if they appear too fibrous.

> **Tasty Morsel** _____
>
> The artichoke is related to the cardoon, another edible thistle. The species originated in the Mediterranean region, probably in what is now Tunisia. In the United States, the modern globe artichoke is grown almost exclusively in the small coastal town of Castroville, California. It's harvested twice a year, in spring and early fall.

Avocado   The avocado is native to the tropics, and its rich, buttery texture and mild nutty flavor have given it the nickname "poor man's butter." The Hass avocado is by far the most popular. It has a dark, thick, wrinkled skin, and the fruit inside is rich and creamy when ripe. The Florida, or Fuerte, variety has a thinner, lighter-green skin, and much denser, often fibrous fruit. Ripe avocados give slightly when squeezed. Plan to purchase your avocado under-ripe and ripen it for a day or two on the counter at home. Avoid bruises, mushy spots, or breaks in the skin. Once cut, avocados will oxidize (turn brown), so leave the cutting until the last minute, or coat lightly with an acidic ingredient such as lemon juice.

Beets   Red garden beets, or beetroots, are firm and bitter raw but tender and sweet when cooked. The greens are edible, too, and are packed with nutrients. Greens wilt quickly and should be removed from the root and eaten with 1 or 2 days of purchase. Roots last 2 or 3 weeks stored in a cool, dry place.

Bok choy   Bok choy, also called pak choi, is often called Chinese cabbage or Chinese chard. You might also find baby bok choy. Bok choy's thick, crunchy, white stalks and tender, green leaves are a characteristic ingredient in much of Asian cuisine. Rather than forming a head, the leaves grow in stalks or blades, much like celery. Even when cooked, the crunchy stalks retain their texture, which is crisp but not at all tough. Look for firm, white stalks and evenly colored, crisp green leaves. Store airtight in the crisper for up to 4 days.

Broccoli   Broccoli is related to cabbage, brussels sprouts, and cauliflower. Look for a crown with tight clusters of tiny buds, dark green, sometimes with a purple tinge at the tips. The stem is edible, too. Eat them as is in young specimens, or peel older broccoli's firm outer skin to reveal the tender inner stem.

You can find several varieties of broccoli at specialty markets or farmers' markets, including romanesco, which is cone-shape and bright green, and purple broccoli, which is brain-shape. Raab, also known as rapini, is grown for its nutty, slightly bitter greens, which look like sprouting broccoli. Broccoli is available year-round, but it's traditionally a cold-weather crop, so the best specimens are available in the fall and winter.

Tasty Morsel

The large cruciferous family of vegetables is a big one and includes cabbage, brussels sprouts, kale, cauliflower, bok choy, collards, mustard greens, cress, and broccoli. In fact, it's the largest crop of edible plants we eat. These vegetables are high in vitamin C and soluble fiber and are rich in nutrients thought to contain anti-cancer properties.

Brussels sprouts   Brussels sprouts grow their tiny heads lined up in rows along a thick stalk. The smaller heads, tight, compact, and 1 or 2 inches in diameter, are the best. Store them no longer than 3 days in the refrigerator, or they'll start turning bitter. Look for red and green varieties at the farmers' market.

Cabbage   Cabbage is a species with much variety. Some come packed in tight heads, while others with loose leaves. Leaves can be purple, green, crinkly, smooth, and shiny. Eaten raw, cabbage is crunchy and fresh, but cooked, it takes on a completely new characteristic. Long used as a staple ingredient, cabbage has been preserved through fermentation in many cultures, in dishes such as sauerkraut and kimchi. Choose firm heads with even coloration, and store airtight in the refrigerator for up to a week.

Carrots   Carrots are an ancient member of the parsley family, which is apparent when you see their lacey green tops. They are high in vitamin A,

Tasty Morsel

Carrots can be seen in Egyptian art from 2000 B.C.E. Carrots of that era weren't orange, but purple and white. The orange carrot didn't appear until the 1400s, when Dutch scientists cultivated a mutant orange seed for the Dutch royal family, the House of Orange.

which is good for vision, and sugar, which explains their mass appeal. They're best eaten when young and slender because they become dry and woody with age. Look for firm, crisp roots, and tops that are moist and bright green. A good scrub is the only preparation a carrot needs, although fat, old, dry carrots may benefit from peeling. Carrots will stay crisp for up to 1 week wrapped in plastic and stored in the vegetable crisper. Perk up wilted carrots in ice water for 30 minutes.

Cauliflower   There are many varieties of cauliflower, including green, purple, brown, and yellow, but the most common cauliflower is white. The head we eat is the floret portion, often called the curd, due to it similarity in appearance to cottage cheese. (It's also affectionately called the brain, for obvious reasons.) Cauliflower is a winter vegetable, and although it's generally available year-round, look for better quality and more variety in the cooler months. Choose firm, compact heads, and keep them wrapped in plastic and refrigerated for up to 4 days.

Celery   Celery is a common ingredient, used in a multitude of ways for its aromatic qualities and hearty crunch. It's also a valuable source of fiber. Chopped and combined with carrots and onions, it becomes the classic *mirepoix*. When slathered with peanut butter, it is the ultimate after school snack.

Lettuce Lingo

Mirepoix is a classic French aromatic ingredient, used in everything from sauces and stews, to braised, poached, and marinated meat and fish. It is made from chopped carrots, onions, celery, and fresh herbs, including parsley and thyme.

Collards   A member of the cabbage family, collards grow in loose leaf bunches rather than heads. They are best at their peak season, in the cold months, but are available year-round in most markets. They're cooked for a long time in traditional southern recipes, but collards can be cooked in the same manner as cabbage as well.

Cucumber The cucumber is a member of the gourd family. The common variety found in most American markets, also known as Persian, has a tough skin and relatively large number of seeds, compared to the English, Mediterranean, and Japanese varieties. Their cool, crisp flesh is best when eaten raw. Some report a problem with burping after consuming cucumber seeds, but they will do you no harm. You can easily remove the seeds by cutting the cuke in half lengthwise and scraping out the seeds with a spoon. Choose firm, heavy cucumbers with bright, even skin. Some grocers wax the outside of their cucumbers to retain moisture. If this is the case, you should probably peel the cucumber. Cucumbers keep nicely in the refrigerator for a week or more.

Eggplant Eggplant can be purple or white, and it comes in a variety of shapes. The name comes from the small egg-shape white eggplant, but the large common eggplant—purple, oblong, and pear-shape—is by far the most recognizable. Japanese eggplant is thin and long and comes in various shades of purple. Italian eggplant is a smaller, more tender version of the common eggplant. Look for heavy fruit that's firm, smooth, and evenly colored. Soft flesh is an indication of age, which means the fruit inside will be bitter. Store eggplants for only a day or two in a cool, dry place.

Green beans Green beans, also known as string beans or snap beans, are the seeded pods of legumes. There are dozens of varieties, including blue lake, golden wax, purple king, and dragon tongue. Fresh green beans can be eaten in the pod, while broad beans, like lima and fava beans, must be shelled before they're eaten.

Kale Another member of the cabbage family, kale has loose, frilly leaves and comes in green and purple varieties. Seen most often as a plate garnish, it can be cooked like spinach, or added to a salad mix. Use fresh, as leaves turn bitter with age. Best in the winter months.

Mustard greens Another member of the cabbage family, mustard greens are often cooked like collards—long and slow. But mustard's peppery flavor is nice sautéed quickly with garlic or added to a salad mix. Look for dark green leaves with tender stems. A winter crop.

Onions Onions were known to the Egyptians and have been coveted in every cuisine worldwide since then. The family also includes garlic, leeks, and shallots. They are all part of the lily family, and if left to grow, these plant yield beautiful flowers that are also edible and make a stunning addition to any salad.

Bulb onions have a round core expanding into layers, with a papery outer skin. They include the red or purple Bermudas, sweet Vidalia and Walla Wallas, common white and yellow, as well as round and elongated shallots. Some onions are valued for their stems. They do not have a rounded bulb, but instead grow a long cylinder of tightly packed leaves. These include the leek, the scallion or green onion, the Welsh onion, and the smallest of the species, the chive, which grows in clumps and includes the Japanese garlic chive Ku chai. The greens and flowers can be harvested from all onions, regardless of their variety.

> **Tasty Morsel**
>
> The pearl onion, also known as the walking onion or tree onion, is a peculiar form. The plant grows a mass of bulbs at the top of the stem, where a normal onion flower would appear.

Unfortunately, when eaten raw, these vegetables tend to linger on the palette. Luckily, you can help combat this side effect by soaking onions in cold water before adding them into a recipe. The harsh oils that offend the breath are leached out, but the flavor stays in. The longer the soak, the better. Potent onions can soak overnight, but be sure to change the water frequently.

Larger onions will make you cry when you chop them. This is a culinary fact of life. The only real way to get around this is to wear goggles, and even that doesn't always work. Mystic voodoo tricks to prevent the tears are yours to try, but my best advice is to chop fast and then cover the chopped onions with plastic wrap when finished.

Store onions, garlic, and shallots in a cool, dry place. It's not necessary to refrigerate them, and in fact, refrigeration tends to convert too much of their starch to sugar, which causes them to burn easily if heated, turning them bitter.

Parsnips   A popular root in Europe, the parsnip is a lonely vegetable in the United States. It looks like a white carrot, with a creamy, sweet texture, and is perfect for purées. They are also well suited for frying, sautéing, and baking. Look for small, firm parsnips in the fall and winter.

Peas   Peas, often called shelling peas when fresh, are quite a treat straight out of the pods. Shelling them isn't hard, and all they need is a 15-second dunk in boiling water, a little salt, and some butter. But fresh shelling peas are rarely available in your local market and only hit the farmers' markets in the late spring and early summer. So for the rest of the year, frozen peas are the best bet.

Heads-Up!
Avoid canned peas with all your might. They are an ugly shade of green, mushy, and have a much different, less-appealing flavor.

Peppers   The pepper family includes both spicy chiles and sweet or bell peppers. They come in a multitude of colors, including pale and dark green, yellow, red, orange, purple, and brown. Sweet peppers, also known as bell peppers, are mild, crisp, and juicy and can range from slightly bitter to sugary sweet. Peppers are available year-round but peak in the summer months. Look for firm peppers that are heavy for their size, with bright color and shiny skin.

Chiles contain capsicum, which is the compound that creates heat you feel in your mouth when you eat chiles. This stuff can create some discomfort, especially on tender, sensitive skin. To be safe, use gloves when chopping chiles, and keep your hands away from your eyes while you're working with chiles.

Potatoes   See Chapter 6 for the dirt on potatoes.

Radishes   Radishes are a spicy little root from a plant in the mustard family. They range in color from the common red to white, pink, purple, black, green, to variegated. They range in spiciness, too, from mild to quite intense, such as horseradish and wasabi, the Japanese condiment made from the exotic green radish. Their shape can be fat and round, oblong, or elongated like a carrot. Choose radishes that are firm and evenly colored. Radishes are usually sold with the greens still attached, so be sure to remove the greens at home, as they deteriorate quickly and will become slimy and smelly very fast.

Summer squash Summer squash is the fruit from a plant in the gourd family. It has thin, edible skin, and includes such common varieties as zucchini, patty pan, and crookneck. The smaller the squash, the sweeter and less bitter it is. Keep summer squash in the refrigerator, well wrapped, for up to 5 days.

Tomatoes Tomatoes come in many varieties, and although they're available year-round, the quality is often less than stellar. It's best to choose tomatoes at the height of their season in the hot months, and look for fresh-off-the-vine tomatoes at farmers' markets. Better yet, grow your own. They're easy to grow, even in pots.

> **Tasty Morsel**
>
> Tomatoes, peppers, and eggplant are all members of the night-shade family. This botanical family contains many species—some that are edible and some that are highly toxic. Because of this, these foods were long considered poisonous. Three cheers to first guy to risk it all for the sake of cuisine!

Pick tomatoes that are dark in color, firm, not mushy, and heavy for their size, which means they are full of juicy goodness. Store them at room temperature for the best flavor. If good tomatoes are unavailable, canned tomatoes can be a good substitute. Picked at the height of the season, their flavor is exceptional, although the texture is much softer.

Winter squash Winter squash is cooked just like the root vegetables and is often included in root vegetable medleys. This category is large and includes pumpkins, butternut, and acorn squashes. Choose a squash that's heavy for its size, with a smooth rind free of blemishes. The thick skin allows for long storage—up to a month or more. The skin and large seeds must be removed. No refrigeration is needed, but they last longer in cool, dark spots.

Helpful Salad-Making Tools

Tools are important for good cooking, and they can determine whether the task is a chore or a pleasure. There are several that are indispensable for salad making—and a few that are just plain fun.

A big bowl is the most important piece of salad-making equipment. You cannot toss a salad adequately if you can't keep the ingredients off the counter. Choose a bowl that's twice as big as the ingredients being tossed. That doesn't mean you have to serve the salad in a giant bowl, though. Toss the salad in the huge bowl first, and transfer it to a decorative serving bowl or platter to serve. This ensures the salad is well tossed and the serving bowl is neat and clean.

Next, a good knife is imperative when you have a lot of chopping to do. One well-made chef knife (also known as a French knife) can last you a lifetime. It has a specific design that, when used properly, makes continuous chopping easy, relatively effortless, and safe.

The key is the curve that runs along the edge from mid-blade to tip. That curve is made for rocking. If you're properly chopping, the tip of the knife should never leave the cutting board. Rock the blade rock down and forward, back and up. The actual cutting should take place toward the rear of the blade.

To hold the knife, grasp the handle. Rest your index finger along the top of the shaft, or wrap it around the handle, whatever's most comfortable for you.

Cut food into manageable lengths, about 3 or 4 inches long. Cut round foods like carrots with a flat edge so they don't rock. Cut them in half lengthwise and lay them on their cut side for stability. Next, slice lengthwise again at desired thickness, to yield several long, flat slices. Lay them flat on their side again, and slice again, lengthwise or crosswise, depending on your desired shape. Most people can cut 2 or 3 pieces of food at a time.

> **Heads-Up!**
> Flashy, showman chefs may chop violently with a lot of noise, but lifting the knife completely off the cutting board with every cut puts enormous tension on the wrist, and after only a few minutes, fatigue can set in.

Once the food is cut, it should be washed and dried, and that's where a salad spinner comes in handy. Salad spinners have revolutionized salad making. Before them, greens had to be air-dried or carefully blotted with a towel. And if the job wasn't done sufficiently, water remaining on the leaves would dilute the dressing.

Today, spinners are easy to come by and greatly speed up the salad-making process. They come in all sizes and styles, so you're sure to find one that fits your needs.

Heads-Up! _____

Watch your fingers! Fingertips are precious, and if you want to keep yours, keep them tucked back, away from the blade, when you're cutting. In the proper position, your fingertips are touching the food, and your first knuckle is pushed forward so it actually comes in contact with the side of the blade. *The* side, *not the* edge, *of the blade!* This contact helps you guide the food into the blade and gives you maximum control over the size of your cuts. This position, with your fingertips back, isn't natural, and will definitely take some practice.

Last but not least, a good box grater is imperative to a well-stocked kitchen. It should have several hole sizes, including a very fine hole for zest grating.

Salad Secret _____

If you're spinner-less, try this old-fashioned trick to dry your greens: open a linen towel and place the greens in the center. Fold towel in half, grasp the ends, and swing it around your head a few times. The centrifugal force will shake the moisture off the leaves, and the towel will catch it.

If you can't find a fine-holed grater, consider the microplane, a carpenter's-rasp-turned-kitchen tool. It's perfect for citrus zest and hard grana cheeses.

The Least You Need to Know

- When making salads, you have dozens of vegetables and fruit varieties to choose from. Try them all to keep a healthy variety of nutrients in your diet!

- Choose bright and colorful fruits and vegetables for a well-rounded selection of vitamins and minerals.

- Fruits and vegetables are best at the height of their season and also offer the highest-quality nutrition then.

- A bowl, knife, spinner, and grater are imperative for efficient salad production.

Chapter 2

Topping It Off

In This Chapter

- ◆ Vinegars for every taste
- ◆ Choosing oil for health and flavor
- ◆ Additional elements to add interest to your salad

There's a joke I love: why was the chef embarrassed? Because he saw the salad dressing! But seriously, make your own dressings? Isn't that hard? Isn't what's in the bottle easier and better tasting? Not necessarily. Dressings are easy to make, delicious, and healthier than anything you can get in a bottle.

There are several types of dressings, and an infinite number of variations. But they all begin with the same basic components: oil and vinegar. To become a terrific dressing chef, it's important to become familiar with these two staple ingredients. Once you discover their potential, you can start experimenting with recipes, and create salads that are uniquely yours.

Versatile Vinegars

Vinegar is a component of nearly every salad dressing. Its purpose is not to make the recipe tart or sour, but to give it balance. Combined with the oil and seasonings, vinegar wakes up the palette and helps create a singular, cohesive flavor. Like salt, the acid in vinegar brightens the natural flavor of foods. It opens the taste buds and makes them more receptive to the dish's flavors.

Choose Your Vinegar

Despite the name, which comes from Old Spanish *vin agre*, meaning "soured wine," vinegar can be made from any liquid that contains alcohol. The alcohol contains ethanol, which oxidizes over a period of weeks, creating sourness. Any fruit juice left at room temperature will oxidize in the same way eventually.

Salad Secret _____

Many cooks are fairly liberal when it comes to adding salt to increase the flavor of a recipe. But a fresh squeeze of lemon or a dash of vinegar often works better. Plus, acid brings a fresher, less chemical flavor—and less sodium.

The recipes in this book call for specific vinegars, but you can find numerous varieties on the market, and all are worth a try. The following table lists some vinegars you might find, along with their characteristics.

Vinegar	Characteristics
White	Made from grain alcohol.
Cider	Made from fermented apple cider.
Malt	Made from malted barley.
Wine	Made from grape wine. Available in red or white, some specific varietals, as well as champagne and sherry.

Vinegar	Characteristics
Balsamic	Made from grape wine, but specifically the white Trebbiano grape that grows on the foothills of Modena, Italy. It is aged in wood over a period of years to create its sweet, distinctively pungent flavor. Highest-quality balsamic can be as thick as syrup.
Fruit	Made from assorted fruit juices, including raspberry, black current, quince, and pomegranate. It can also be made by soaking fruit in wine vinegar for several weeks.
Rice	Made from fermented rice. Also called rice wine vinegar.

Flavored Vinegars

A great way to add interest to your salad is to create your own vinegar. Infused vinegars are easy to make and can feature specific flavors of herbs and spices.

When making flavored vinegar, it's best to start with a vinegar that's light in flavor. Distilled white vinegar is too harsh, but white wine vinegar is a good choice, as is rice vinegar. Cider vinegar can work, too, if the spices and herbs are strong in flavor. Red wine and balsamic vinegar are generally too strong, and their flavor tends to compete with infusions.

Be sure you thoroughly clean and sanitize both the herbs and the jars when making flavored vinegar to help prevent E. coli contamination. A run through the dishwasher will do the trick for the jars.

To wash the herbs, submerge them in cold water, swish them around, then drain and dry.

To ensure no harmful bacteria are present, bring your vinegar to a simmer before pouring it into a sanitized jar packed with clean, chopped herbs and spices. Cover it loosely with cheesecloth or a clean towel. When completely cool, seal it with a sterilized lid and set it in a cool, dark spot for 2 to 4 weeks to infuse.

When you think the vinegar is ready, strain out the herbs and taste the vinegar. If it's not strong enough, repeat the process with a new batch of clean, chopped herbs. If it tastes ready, strain out any small particles and cloudiness through a coffee filter or several layers of cheesecloth. Place a few decorative sprigs of clean herbs inside a sanitized decorative bottle, and pour in the flavored vinegar. Seal with a sanitized cork or cap.

> **Heads-Up!**
>
> Be sure the bottle seal is not made of metal or rubber, which are both easily corroded by acid.

You can use a single herb or spice to create a terrific flavored vinegar or use a combination. These vinegars not only enhance your salad dressings, but they can stand alone as a dressing, glaze, marinade, or dip.

If you're stuck for a flavored vinegar idea, try one of the herb and spice combinations in the following table.

Flavored Vinegar	Ingredients
Garden Herb	4 parts parsley; 3 parts chives; 2 parts each thyme, tarragon; 1 part each sage, celery seed; white wine vinegar
Chile Spice	3 parts dried chile flakes; 2 parts each coriander, cumin; 1 part each garlic, thyme, oregano, cumin; cider vinegar
Mint	2 parts each peppermint, spearmint; 1 part each lemon zest, anise seed; 1 part sugar; rice vinegar
Winter Spice	2 parts each rosemary, thyme; 1 part each mint, allspice berries, chopped ginger, cardamom; 1 cinnamon stick; 3 cloves; $1/4$ vanilla bean; white wine vinegar
Eastern	3 parts each lime zest, cilantro, scallion; 2 parts toasted sesame seed; 1 part each chopped garlic, chopped ginger, star anise, Szechwan peppercorns; rice vinegar
Fruit	3 parts raspberries; 1 part each basil, lemon zest, thyme; 1 cinnamon stick; white wine vinegar

Outstanding Oils

Oil is an important element in cooking because it carries flavor. Have you ever gotten oil on your hands? Did you notice that it spread quickly onto everything it touched? It does this in your recipes, too. Everything that touches the oil becomes oily. If that oil contains flavorful elements, then everything it touches receives that flavor, too.

On a salad, oil is crucial. Without oil, the dressing would slide off the greens and pool at the bottom of the bowl, taking all the flavors with it.

Oils and Fats

Oils and fats go by the chemical name *lipids*. Lipids, found in both plants and animals, are important nutrients and provide a concentrated source of energy and calories. Fat is needed to transport fat-soluble vitamins, insulate you in winter, and cushion your vital organs. But as you probably know, you don't need very much of it. For good health, it's important to understand and choose the right kind of fat.

Saturated fats are found mainly in animal-based foods like meat, butter, cheese, and lard. They can easily be identified because they're solid at room temperature. While saturated fats are found mainly in animal products, there are two exceptions: palm oil and coconut oil. These fats are solid at room temperature and trans-fat free. They're easier for your body to absorb than trans fat, and coconut oil especially is often used in place of partially hydrogenated vegetable oils.

 Tasty Morsel

> You can tell fats and oils apart because, in general, when stored at room temperature, fat is solid and oil is liquid.

Saturated fats are considered the most dangerous types of fat because they appear to raise blood cholesterol levels. They also may inhibit the liver's ability to clear out low density lipoproteins (LDL, or bad cholesterol) and may actually increase the production of LDL. The result is an increased likelihood of atherosclerosis and coronary artery disease.

Unsaturated fats are liquid at room temperature. They're generally referred to as oils, and they come mainly from plant sources. There are two types of unsaturated fats: *monounsaturated* and *polyunsaturated*. Monounsaturated fats occur in olive, canola, and nut oils, including peanut oil. Polyunsaturated fats include plant oils like safflower, sunflower, cottonseed, sesame, corn, and soybean. Unsaturated fats have been shown to actually lower the bad cholesterol (LDL) in your blood.

Polyunsaturated fats are the "omegas." *Omega-3* and *omega-6* are essential fatty acids. *Essential* means we need to get them through our food because our body cannot manufacture them.

Omega-3 is found in fish oil and plant oils, especially flax. It's believed to reduce inflammation, improve blood circulation, and decrease the thickness of arterial walls—a significant benefit to those with high blood serum cholesterol. Omega-6 is found in nuts, whole grains, legumes, sesame oil, and soy oil. When used together to replace saturated fats, these fatty acids can reduce high blood pressure and cholesterol.

Heads-Up!

Unsaturated fats have a shorter shelf life and are more likely to turn rancid, thanks to the culprits oxygen and light. Store oil in a cool, dark place. For long-term storage, use the refrigerator.

But trans fat is now known to both lower the good cholesterol and raise the bad. Even worse, in recent years, trans fats have been used extensively in manufactured foods.

All About Olive Oil

Olive oil is the most popular oil for salad making, so it gets its own special mention.

The olive tree has been cultivated for at least 6,000 years. The fruit has always been preferred more for its oil, not only for cooking but also for cosmetics, soap, and fuel. Olive trees are still highly valued, and some living, fruiting specimens are upward of 1,000 years old.

Black and green olives come from the same tree but are harvested at different stages and processed in different ways. Under-ripe olives are always green. Ripe olives range from deep green to purple-black. Fresh olives must be fermented to remove their natural bitterness. This is done by first soaking them in lye and then in brine, or dry-cured, to soften and infuse flavors.

To make oil, ripe olives are ground to a paste between millstones and then pressed. (Only perfectly ripe olives yield a good-flavored oil. If the olive is too young, the flavor will be bitter. If it is too old, the oil will be rancid.) The initial oil exuded is considered the highest quality. *Virgin oil* refers to oil manufactured with no chemical treatment. *Refined oil* has been chemically treated to neutralize acid and balance flavor.

The following table gives you the types and characteristics of different olive oils, listed from highest to lowest quality.

Olive Oil	Characteristics
Extra-virgin	Cold pressed, chemical free, with no more than .80 percent acidity. The first pressing of the olives generally yields naturally low acidity and a rich fruit color and flavor.
Virgin	Also chemical free, from the first cold pressing, but with acidity less than 2 percent.
Fino	A blend of extra-virgin and virgin olive oils, with acidity less than 2 percent.
Pure/olive oil	A blend of virgin and refined oil, with no more than 1.5 percent acidity.
Light olive oil	Another blend of virgin and refined oil, with no more than 1.5 percent acidity, but filtered to remove color and fragrance. It's not lighter in fat or calories.

Flavored Oils

Oils infused with the flavors of herbs and spices are a fun way to add interest to salads. The method is similar to that of vinegar, but you must take some precautions during the preparation.

Acidic vinegar is an inhospitable environment for botulism, a potentially lethal paralytic disease. However, a little moisture trapped in an oxygen-free bottle of oil is a perfect host. Sanitizing the bottles and herbs is an important step, but that's just the first step. Take care to completely dry foods you plan to infuse into the oil. Oil with infusions of foods with a lot of internal moisture, like garlic or chiles, are especially susceptible to botulism. Make these oils in small batches and store them in the refrigerator.

To accentuate the flavors of the spices and herbs in your oil, choose a neutral oil as your base. Use one that has a very light flavor, such as canola, safflower, or vegetable oil.

Unlike infused vinegars, oil should not be heated before it's infused. Pour it cool into a sanitized jar of clean spices and chopped herbs. Seal it tightly with a sanitized lid, and let it sit in a cool dark spot for 2 weeks. Shake the jar daily to blend the aromatic oils with the base oil. After 2 weeks, taste the oil. If the flavor is lacking, strain the oil into another sterilized jar full of spices and herbs, and repeat the process.

Use your infused oil for salads, drizzle it over grilled meat and seafood, use it for roasted vegetables, or simply dip in some good, crusty bread.

Flavored Oil	Ingredients
Herbaceous Olive	2 parts each rosemary, basil, sage; 1 part each chopped garlic, fennel seed, basil; olive oil
Spicy Barbecue	2 parts each oregano, thyme, cilantro; 1 part each cumin, coriander, chile arbol, lime zest, brown sugar, garlic, mustard seed; 1 cinnamon stick; peanut oil
Savory (for seafood)	2 parts each bay leaves, celery seeds; 1 part each cardamom, allspice, chopped ginger; 1 vanilla bean; 1 cinnamon stick; corn oil
Lemon Pepper	Zest of 3 lemons; 1 part each pink peppercorn, Szechwan peppercorn, chopped ginger; corn oil

Flavored Oil	Ingredients
Caribbean	2 parts each juniper berries, cilantro, thyme; 1 part each chopped garlic, chopped ginger; 1 scotch bonnet chile; 1 cinnamon stick; peanut oil

Styles of Dressings

Salad dressings come in a few basic types. The flavors and ingredients may vary, but the basic structure remains the same. So when you understand the basics, creating your own interpretation is a snap.

Vinaigrettes

As the name implies, a vinaigrette typically contains vinegar, but not always. The name also gives you a hint of the flavor, but a vinaigrette should not be overpoweringly sour. There must be balance. The purpose if this type of dressing is to accentuate the flavor of the vegetables it coats, not hide it.

There are several recipes for vinaigrette, but they all stem from a classic 3:1 ratio of oil to vinegar, as you'll see by the Classic French Vinaigrette recipe later in this chapter. Any oil and any acidic ingredient can be used to create a unique version of the vinaigrette. Throughout the recipes in this book, you'll see variations on this theme.

Tasty Morsel

It's widely believed that eating vinegar at the start of a meal helps stimulate your appetite. This reason? The increased salivation the acid causes gets your stomach working.

A characteristic trait of the vinaigrette is its inability to stay mixed. Because the vinegar is mostly water, it won't mix with the oil. Therefore, the two ingredients must be mixed just prior to dressing and serving. One popular method involves combining the dressing ingredients in a jar with a tight-fitting lid and shaking it vigorously before adding it to a salad. This method, too, enables you to add on just the right amount.

Emulsified Dressings

Unlike the vinaigrette, the *emulsified* dressing was designed to get vinegar and oil to mix ... and then stay together.

Emulsification is the blending of two ingredients by suspension of small globules of one inside the other, so that the resulting blend becomes one homogeneous substance. This can only occur with the help of an emulsifying ingredient, which is usually lecithin. Lecithin is a lipid found naturally in soy and egg yolks. Soy lecithin is used widely in manufacturing, but it's the humble egg yolk that helps us in our home kitchens.

Heads-Up!

Don't be alarmed by the appearance of an egg yolk in this type of recipe. Yolks are necessary and have been used for centuries to create emulsified dressings. If your eggs are chilled, and you, your equipment, and your kitchen are clean, there is no danger. Most people worry that raw eggs will give them salmonella, but actually, the majority of salmonella cases are caused by unwashed fruit, not raw eggs or meat.

The classic emulsified dressing is mayonnaise, and if you like the store-bought kind, just wait until you try it homemade. This technique is easier than you think—as you'll see with the Classic Mayonnaise dressing later in this chapter—and when you master it, you can create some fabulous dressings and dips with the addition of just a few more ingredients. For instance, add 2 or 3 mashed or roasted garlic cloves for classic aioli. Add some paprika, chili sauce, and onion for a sensational Thousand Island. Blue cheese, Worcestershire, and a little white wine vinegar make a great blue cheese dressing. There are no rules. Just let your imagination carry you away.

Creamy Dressings

You'd think that creamy dressings are defined by the addition of cream, but they can include any other creamy ingredient, usually a dairy product, such as sour cream, yogurt, or buttermilk, or combination, as you'll see in the Classic Cream Dressing recipe later in this chapter.

Creamy dressings are cool and light yet still thick enough to thoroughly coat the salad ingredients. Creamy dressings can be savory like ranch dressing or sweet like a yogurt dressing meant for fruit salad.

On Top: Croutons and Nuts

A crunchy element is welcome atop any salad. The standard toasted cubes of bread are easy to make or buy, but don't stop there. Anything crisp can serve in this role, even nuts.

To make standard *croutons*, use old bread, or cube fresh bread and let it dry out at room temperature for 1 or 2 days. (The absence of moisture in a crouton makes it crunchy and allows the bread to absorb more flavor from the dressing and other ingredients.) When they're dry, toss the bread cubes in oil and seasonings and toast them. You can easily vary the breads, oils, and seasonings to suit your recipe, or simply to use any leftover bread you have on hand. Check out the Basic Croutons recipe later in this chapter.

Lettuce Lingo

Crouton is a French name for a thin toasted piece of bread. In classic French cuisine, it's typically large and thin and more likely to appear floating on soup than tossed in a salad. But thanks to Caesar Cardini and his salad, the American crouton is more often shaped in small cubes and tossed among the greens.

There are other ways to add a crouton-esque crunchiness to your salads. Cut into triangles and baked, pita chips make great croutons, as well as fun snack food. Tortilla strips and wonton wrappers can be baked, too, or fried lightly in oil. A number of fun, ready-made foods add interesting texture to salads, like crispy chow mein noodles, pretzels, chips, and even cereal such as shredded wheat and granola. When looking for a crunchy salad element, let the style and origin of the recipe be your guide.

And then we have nuts. Nuts are crunchy, flavorful, and nutritious. They come in many varieties, and you can find one to suit any cuisine.

Nuts are much better when toasted. The heat extracts the flavorful oils and intensifies the flavor. The best method of toasting nuts is to roast them. The all-around heat browns them evenly, unlike toasting in a sauté pan, where only the portion touching the pan gets brown, and the nuts can easily burn. Roasting nuts is easy. Spread them in a single layer on a baking sheet, and bake at 350°F for 5 to 10 minutes or until they're fragrant and toasted. Shake them around periodically to ensure even browning.

> **Heads-Up!**
>
> Because nuts are high in oil, they turn rancid if stored at room temperature for a prolonged period. Avoid this by storing them in the refrigerator or the freezer if you plan to keep them for more than a week.

Tossing It All Together

Everyone has his or her own taste preferences. Some like the fresh taste of veggies lightly enhanced by a flavorful dressing. Others are accustomed to a thick coating of dressing on their vegetables. For the best results, strive for a light coating. The goal is to enhance the natural flavor of the veggies, not hide them. Regardless of your personal taste, as a host, it's better to underdress your salad and let the guests ask for more dressing if they want more.

Of course, no amount of dressing does a salad any good if it's not properly tossed in. The first rule of tossing a salad is to be sure all your greens are dry. If they're not, the dressing will be diluted. Use a good salad spinner, or blot the leaves with paper or linen towels.

Next, use an oversize bowl. No good tossing can occur if the ingredients are tossed out onto the counter. Tongs are a great utensil for tossing because you can grasp and turn the greens while simultaneously turning and tilting the bowl. Clean hands are the best tool of all, but you can only use them when you're alone in your kitchen. (No one wants to see you do that.) Whatever you use, toss for a good long time to be sure the dressing has thoroughly coated all the vegetables.

Finally, serve your tossed salad right away. A dressed dressing deteriorates rapidly. If you have a lot of cooking to do, prepare the vegetables and dressing separately, keep them chilled, and combine them at the last minute.

Classic French Vinaigrette

This standard recipe should be fresh and light, not too tart or acidic. Personalize it with your choice of fresh herbs.

1 TB. white wine vinegar

1 TB. lemon juice

6 TB. olive oil

Pinch kosher salt

Pinch white pepper

¼ tsp. dry mustard

1 TB. fresh parsley, chive, tarragon, or your herb of choice, chopped

Yield: ½ **cup dressing**
Prep time: 5 minutes
Serving size: 2 table-spoons

1. In a medium bowl, whisk together white wine vinegar, lemon juice, olive oil, salt, pepper, dry mustard, and herbs.

2. Use immediately to dress a salad or refrigerate several weeks for later use.

Salad Secret

Instead of whisking in a bowl, you can combine this dressing in a jar with a tight-fitting lid and shake it up.

Classic Mayonnaise

Homemade mayonnaise is never oily or greasy. Add enough lemon juice to cut through the fat for a clean but neutral flavor.

1 egg yolk

2 tsp. lemon juice

1 tsp. water

½ tsp. dry mustard

1 cup canola oil

Pinch kosher salt

Pinch white pepper

> **Yield: 2½ cups mayonnaise**
>
> **Prep time:** 15 minutes
>
> **Serving size:** 1 tablespoon

1. In a large bowl, whisk together egg yolk, lemon juice, water, and dry mustard until foamy.

2. Slowly drizzle in canola oil while whisking.

3. Season with salt and pepper, and add a little more lemon juice if necessary.

4. Store in the refrigerator for up to 2 weeks.

 Salad Secret

If your bowl tends to spin on the countertop while you whisk, try this trick: place the bowl on a wet towel. This will hold it still.

Classic Cream Dressing

Buttermilk provides the characteristic tang to this herby recipe. If you'd like an extra tangy kick, replace the buttermilk with plain yogurt.

¾ cup sour cream

1¼ cup buttermilk

1 TB. Dijon mustard

2 TB. white wine vinegar

1 TB. lemon juice

1 clove garlic, minced

1 scallion, minced

1 TB. chopped fresh parsley

½ tsp. celery seed

> **Yield: about 2½ cups**
>
> **Prep time:** 5 minutes
>
> **Serving size:** 2 table-spoons

1. In a large bowl, whisk together sour cream, buttermilk, and Dijon mustard.

2. Add white wine vinegar, lemon juice, garlic, scallion, parsley, and celery seed, and stir to combine.

3. Store in the refrigerator for up to 1 week.

Salad Secret

For a little extra tang, replace the sour cream with plain yogurt.

Basic Croutons

Garlicky, crispy, and light, these fresh croutons add the perfect touch.

3 cloves garlic, chopped

¼ cup olive oil

1 TB. dried thyme

4 cups stale French bread, cut in small cubes and dried

Yield: 4 cups
Prep time: 15 minutes, plus 12 to 24 hours to dry bread
Cook time: 30 minutes
Serving size: ¼ cup

1. Preheat the oven to 325°F.

2. In a small sauté pan over medium heat, cook garlic in olive oil for 1 or 2 minutes or until golden.

3. Strain into a large bowl, and discard garlic. Add thyme and bread cubes, and toss thoroughly.

Salad Secret

You can make croutons from any bread. Try using a healthful whole-grain or hearty rye bread.

4. Spread bread cubes on a baking sheet in a single layer, and bake for 15 to 20 minutes or until toasted, tossing occasionally for even browning.

5. Cool and then use immediately, or store in the freezer for up to 1 week.

Part 2

Salads on the Side

Salads can take many roles in a meal, but the most common is as a supporting player. Before a meal, or alongside one, is the salad's most beloved performance.

The chapters in Part 2 introduce recipes for classic salads to accompany every possible type of meal. Here you find fresh and light salads with greens and vegetable, both warm and cold. There are standard picnic and potluck recipes; interesting twists on old favorites; and even fruit salads for breakfast, brunch, and lunch.

Chapter 3

Green Salads

In This Chapter

- Fresh and healthful tossed greens
- Great classic salads and everyday favorites
- Modern and delicious flavor combinations

Ancient people saw the health benefits of fresh herbs and vegetables long before it became a first course. The term *salad* comes from Latin *herba salata*, which means "salted herb," a common Roman preparation of lettuce and herbs.

Medieval recipes extol the healing properties of lettuces and herbs, and Renaissance chefs believed that adding vinegar to a dressing stimulated the appetite for things to come. Modern chefs of the Nouveau era favored the cleansing properties of greens, clearing and preparing the palette for an onslaught of new tastes and courses. Today, the green salad is one of the few healthful elements of a typical American meal, and one of the few ways we eat our veggies.

Salads are just as likely to make their appearance as the main course as the first course, especially when the weather warms up. Salads have become an important element of entertaining, barbecues, potlucks, and buffets. But whether you serve it in a big, beautiful bowl or on a separate plate, green salads are a welcome addition to any meal.

Delicate Leaves

Most people consider several types of leaf vegetables as "lettuce." (See Chapter 1 for an extensive list.) The darker leaves are always the most nutritious, as they have a greater concentration of vitamins and minerals. Choose greens that are crisp and bright, with a minimum of wilted or bruised leaves.

> **Heads-Up!**
> You can discard some outer leaves, but throwing too many away can be a waste of money.

Many lettuces are quite dirty, having grown in moist, sandy soil, so when you get them home, give your loose-leaf heads two or three deep soakings in clean, cool water. Allow them to drain thoroughly, or give them a spin in a salad spinner. Excess water on the leaves can dilute your salad dressing.

Don't wash leaves in advance, because water causes them to wilt sooner. Store your lettuce unwashed in the crisper drawer of your refrigerator, wrapped loosely in plastic, until you're ready for it.

All lettuce greens are delicate and perishable. Like other fruits and vegetables, lettuce leaves can bruise. If you cut up your greens too far in advance, the edges will brown. To reduce bruising, chop them just before use, or try ripping the leaves gently.

House Salad

Of course, you can name any salad your house salad, but traditionally the house salad is a simple affair of crunchy, mild greens, minimal veggies, and a tangy vinaigrette, as this one is.

1 clove garlic

1 tsp. Dijon mustard

3 TB. red wine vinegar

½ cup olive oil

¼ cup chopped fresh parsley

¼ tsp. kosher salt

¼ tsp. freshly ground black pepper

½ head iceberg lettuce, chopped

¼ cup purple cabbage, chopped

1 cup croutons

1 medium cucumber, sliced

1 cup cherry tomatoes, halved

> **Yield: 1 large salad**
>
> **Prep time:** 20 minutes
>
> **Serving size:** ¼ salad

1. In a small bowl, whisk together garlic, Dijon mustard, red wine vinegar, olive oil, parsley, kosher salt, and pepper.

2. In a large salad bowl, combine iceberg lettuce, purple cabbage, and croutons. Drizzle dressing on top, and toss thoroughly to coat.

3. Divide salad evenly among plates. Garnish with sliced cucumbers and cherry tomatoes, and serve.

Salad Secret

If your cucumbers or cherry tomatoes are less than perfect, forget them and use whatever's fresh and in season. Or consider using pickled or dried vegetables, like people did before refrigeration.

Iceberg Wedge

This elegant recipe is a throwback to simpler times. The crisp iceberg has a welcome texture on a hot day, and it's the perfect precursor to a richer meal.

¼ lb. blue cheese

2 TB. balsamic vinegar

3 TB. olive oil

¼ tsp. kosher salt

1 tsp. freshly *cracked* black pepper

1 head iceberg lettuce, quartered and cored

Yield: 4 small salads

Prep time: 10 minutes

Serving size: 1 salad

1. In a small bowl, combine blue cheese, balsamic vinegar, olive oil, kosher salt, and pepper. Mix well, smashing cheese with a fork. Set aside.

2. Place each wedge of iceberg on a plate, and drizzle with dressing. Top with additional pepper as needed, and serve.

Lettuce Lingo

Cracked pepper is thicker and rougher than ground pepper. To make it, place the peppercorns on a cutting board and press them firmly with the back of a skillet.

Italian Green Salad

It's not just the color that makes this salad Italian; it's also the seasoning, which is a classic Italian blend of spices. Paired with tomatoes, basil, and Parmesan cheese, it tastes like Rome.

2 cloves garlic

2 TB. red wine vinegar

1/2 tsp. dried oregano

1/2 tsp. fennel seed, ground

1/2 tsp. dried sage

3 TB. olive oil

2 cups romaine lettuce, chopped

3 cups red leaf lettuce, chopped

1 cup fresh basil leaves

2 large tomatoes, sliced in wedges

1/4 cup *Parmesan cheese*, grated

Yield: 4 small salads

Prep time: 20 minutes

Serving size: 1 salad

1. In a small bowl, whisk together garlic, red wine vinegar, oregano, fennel seed, sage, and olive oil.

2. In a large salad bowl, combine romaine lettuce, red leaf lettuce, and basil leaves. Drizzle on dressing, and toss thoroughly to coat.

3. Divide among serving plates. Garnish with tomatoes and Parmesan cheese, and serve.

Lettuce Lingo

Parmesan cheese is the classic hard or granular cheese named for the Parma region in Lombardy, Italy, where is it produced. Buy it whole and grate it yourself for the best results.

Caesar Salad

This is the classic salty, crunchy salad and its famous creamy dressing.

1 egg yolk

1 clove garlic, minced

4 anchovy fillets, minced

3 TB. lemon juice

¼ cup olive oil

Salt and pepper

1 head romaine lettuce, washed, dried, and chopped

½ cup freshly grated Parmesan cheese

1 cup garlic croutons

12 whole anchovy fillets

Yield: 4 small salads

Prep time: 20 minutes

Serving size: 1 salad

1. In a large bowl, whisk together egg yolk, garlic, minced anchovies, and lemon juice. Slowly drizzle in olive oil while whisking, taking 3 or 4 minutes to add all oil. Season with salt and pepper.

2. Add romaine lettuce, Parmesan cheese, and croutons. Toss well to coat, and divide among 4 plates. Top each salad with 3 whole anchovy filets, and serve.

Tasty Morsel _____

This salad was first created in the 1920s by Tijuana restaurateur Caesar Cardini and was traditionally made tableside, assembled right before your very eyes by skilled waiters. You can do this for your guests, too. Get a nice big wooden bowl, and build the salad from the dressing up. And don't be alarmed by the raw egg yolk in this recipe. Yolks are necessary to create an emulsified dressing. If your eggs are chilled, and you, your equipment, and your kitchen are clean, there's no danger. In fact, the majority of salmonella cases are caused by unwashed fruit (usually melons), not raw eggs or meat

Classic Spinach Salad

Popeye loved the iron, but it's the fresh taste of spring we love in spinach. Paired with the classic garnish of mushrooms, eggs, and bacon, you can't miss with this favorite.

1 clove garlic, minced

1 tsp. Dijon mustard

1/2 cup olive oil

3 TB. red wine vinegar

1/4 tsp. kosher salt

1/4 tsp. freshly ground black pepper

1 bunch spinach, washed, dried, and deveined

3 eggs, hard-boiled and sliced

8 to 10 white mushrooms, sliced

1 red onion, sliced

6 slices bacon, fried crisp and crumbled

1 cup chopped toasted pecans

> **Yield: 1 large salad**
> **Prep time:** 20 minutes
> **Serving size:** 1/4 salad

1. In a small bowl, whisk together garlic, Dijon mustard, olive oil, red wine vinegar, salt, and pepper. Set aside.

2. In a large salad bowl, combine dried spinach, egg, mushrooms, onion, and bacon. Drizzle on enough dressing to lightly coat greens, and toss. Serve topped with toasted pecans.

Heads-Up!

Be sure to wash the spinach well. It generally needs two or three rinses to get rid of all the its sandy soil.

Mixed Asian Spinach with Peanut Dressing

This recipe puts a twist on the classic spinach salad with an exotic splash of ginger, sesame, and peanut.

2 cloves garlic

1 TB. fresh ginger, grated

1 tsp. sesame seeds

2 TB. peanut butter

1 TB. honey

3 TB. sherry vinegar

1 TB. sesame oil

2 TB. vegetable oil

4 cups spinach leaves, wash, dried, and deveined

2 cups *bok choy*, shredded

1 red bell pepper, ribs and seeds removed, and sliced

5 or 6 radishes, sliced

½ cup peanuts, chopped

| **Yield: 1 large salad** |
| **Prep time:** 20 minutes |
| **Serving size:** ¼ salad |

1. In a small bowl, whisk together garlic, ginger, sesame seeds, peanut butter, honey, sherry vinegar, sesame oil, and vegetable oil.

2. In a large salad bowl, combine spinach, bok choy, red bell pepper, and radishes. Drizzle on enough dressing to lightly coat greens, and toss thoroughly. Serve topped with chopped peanuts.

> **Lettuce Lingo**
>
> **Bok choy** (also known as bok choi, bak choi, paak choi, and Chinese cabbage) is related to the common turnip and has been cultivated for at least 6,000 years. It looks a little like chard, with big, thick, crunchy white ribs. It's a good source of calcium and vitamins A and C.

Spinach-Pecan Salad

With the crunchy pecans and chewy tart cranberries, this salad tastes like autumn.

2 TB. Dijon mustard

2 TB. balsamic vinegar

2 TB. honey

¼ tsp. kosher salt

¼ tsp. freshly ground black pepper

3 TB. olive oil

4 cups spinach leaves, washed, dried, and deveined

1 cup pecan halves, toasted

½ cup dried cranberries

Yield: 1 large salad
Prep time: 20 minutes
Serving size: ¼ salad

1. In a small bowl, whisk together Dijon mustard, balsamic vinegar, honey, kosher salt, pepper, and olive oil.

2. In a large salad bowl, place spinach. Drizzle on enough dressing to thoroughly coat leaves, and toss. Top with pecans and cranberries, and serve.

Salad Secret

You can purchase spinach in bags, already washed and deveined, and ready to use. This saves time but costs more. And bagged spinach has a very short shelf life after it's been opened.

Baby Greens Salad

This elegant salad is easy as pie and guaranteed to impress. The mix of mild, sweet, bitter, and spicy greens is delightfully fresh and herbaceous.

Zest and juice of 1 lemon (about 2 TB.)

$\frac{1}{2}$ tsp. kosher salt

$\frac{1}{2}$ tsp. freshly ground black pepper

1 TB. Dijon mustard

$\frac{1}{2}$ cup olive oil

4 cups mixed greens

Yield: 1 large salad

Prep time: 10 minutes

Serving size: $\frac{1}{4}$ salad

1. In a small bowl, whisk together lemon zest, lemon juice, kosher salt, pepper, Dijon mustard, and olive oil. Set aside.

2. In a large salad bowl, place greens. Drizzle on enough dressing to lightly coat, and toss. Serve immediately.

Salad Secret

Baby greens are available in most supermarkets, often prewashed, but if you'd rather mix your own, use a variety of colors, textures, and flavors. Mild butter or romaine; spicy arugula, mustard, or dandelion; bitter curly or Belgian endive; and colorful radicchio or nasturtium petals are all great choices.

Arugula-Walnut Salad with Blue Cheese Croutons

The slight peppery tang of arugula is a lovely match to hearty roasted walnuts. The addition of sweet honey and the salty blue cheese makes this salad an explosion of flavors.

2 shallots, minced

Zest and juice of 1 lemon

1 TB. honey

¼ tsp. kosher salt

¼ tsp. freshly ground black pepper

4 TB. walnut oil

1 cup walnuts, toasted and chopped

4 cups arugula

½ French baguette, sliced thin at an angle, and toasted

¼ cup blue cheese

Yield: 1 large salad
Prep time: 20 minutes
Cook time: 10 minutes
Serving size: ¼ salad

1. Preheat the oven to 375°F.

2. In a small bowl, whisk together shallots, lemon zest, lemon juice, honey, kosher salt, pepper, walnut oil, and walnuts.

3. Brush baguette slices lightly with dressing, and spread with blue cheese. Place on a baking sheet, and bake for 5 to 8 minutes or until golden brown. Cool.

4. In a large salad bowl, toss together arugula with enough dressing to lightly coat greens. Serve with blue cheese croutons.

Tasty Morsel

Arugula, also known as rocket or roquette, has been a popular salad green since ancient Roman times. Its seeds were also used medicinally, most notably in aphrodisiacs.

Chapter 4

Vegetable Salads

In This Chapter

- ◆ Marinated, shredded, and roasted vegetable salads
- ◆ Tangy, sweet, and simple dressings
- ◆ Crunchy and creamy salads

Sure, lettuce is a vegetable. But in this chapter, we sample salad recipes made with every vegetable that *isn't* lettuce. You name it—if it's a vegetable, it can be used to make a salad. Just keep it cool, dress it artfully, and voilà! Salad!

Vegetable Prep Tips

Wash all vegetables thoroughly before adding them to a salad. In most cases, a good rinse with water and a gentle wipe does the trick. There's really no need for fancy food washes. Occasionally, though, a little more is called for. Veggies that grow underground or have a lot of crevices may require a short soak. Really dirty roots benefit from a good scrub with a sturdy brush.

The nutrients in most vegetables are concentrated near the skin, so peeling off the skin reduces the vegetables' nutritional value. Whenever possible, eat the skin.

Root Vegetables and Squash

Potatoes, winter squash, and other root vegetables cook better and retain more nutrients when they're cooked in their skins. Just be sure to scrub them free of dirt before cooking them.

Boiling is the most common way to cook roots, but it's not ideal for salad making. Not only are nutrients leached into the water (and thus lost), but the roots absorb a great deal of water as they cook, which makes them soggy and mushy. Then, as they sit in your salad bowl, the water seeps out and thins out your dressing.

A better alternative is roasting. The oven's dry heat evaporates the water in the roots, making them dry, soft, and ready to absorb the dressing. There's no special technique to this method. Simply wrap the roots loosely in foil and bake them at a fairly high temperature such as 375° to 400°F until tender. Allow to cool completely, and peel or dice as necessary.

Onions

Most people agree that, although they may love eating raw onions, they do not love the taste and smell of their breath afterward! Soaking sliced raw onions in cold water reduces the offensive onion oils that make eating onions a bummer for you and those around you.

Soak onions as long as you can, and overnight if possible. (Note that prolonged soaking requires changing the water every few hours.) Even if you can only soak them for 30 minutes, you'll be amazed at the improvement in the onions' taste and aftertaste.

Beans

Fresh string beans need very little preparation. If they have a firm stem attached, trim it off. Beans have a string attached to the stem that runs the length of the bean. In older beans, this string is thick and fibrous and should be removed. It's barely noticeable in tender young beans.

Fresh *legumes* such as peas, fava beans, black-eyed peas, or soybeans need little more than shelling.

Cook dried beans, also called *pulses*, before using them. Soak them overnight, drain, and boil in fresh water for 2 or 3 hours or until tender. Don't salt dried beans until they're fully cooked because salt toughens them. If you'd prefer to avoid this rigmarole, canned beans are a perfectly acceptable option.

Lettuce Lingo

A **legume** is the plant species that has seeds found inside a long seed pod. In culinary language, *legume* refers to the fresh seed from the pod. When that seed is dried, it's known as a **pulse**.

Mushrooms

Mushrooms often contain a lot of dirt, and should be washed. Some chefs believe a mushroom should just be brushed clean and never washed, because mushrooms act like a sponge and soak up water, which can seep out into a recipe.

However, this effect occurs mainly in older mushrooms that have been sitting around a while. As mushrooms age, the underside of their cap opens, exposing the porous gills. Fresh mushrooms, still closed under the cap, absorb very little moisture and can be washed.

Tips for Cooking Vegetables

Many vegetables can, and should, be used raw in salads, because as soon as heat is applied, vegetables start to lose their nutrients. But some veggies such as green beans, asparagus, broccoli, and brussels sprouts, as well as roots such as beets and potatoes, simply better cooked. The trick is to cook them just enough, and never too much.

Blanching, also called parboiling, is a method of precooking vegetables that works well to preserve texture, color, and nutrients. The trick is to pay attention while you work. Drop veggies into boiling water and cook them only for 2 or 3 minutes or until their color is bright and the texture is *al dente*. Then immediately drain and plunge them into ice water. This stops the cooking, keeps them at their brightest color, and leaves them with the best texture for salads.

> **Lettuce Lingo**
>
> *Al dente* is an Italian term that means "to the tooth" and refers to the degree to which certain foods, usually pasta and vegetables, are cooked. These foods are cooked until done but still have slight texture when bitten. They're not raw, crunchy, or soft

The Benefits of Canned and Frozen Veggies

Although fresh produce is always healthier and tastier, seasons and location don't always make fresh possible. Luckily, modern technology enables us to enjoy foods from all over the globe, all year long.

Canned vegetables are cooked by the canning process, which usually renders them mushy. In salads, this texture isn't what you want for veggies like asparagus or peas, but it's fine for firmer veggies such as beans, artichoke hearts, and corn. Canned vegetables are packed in salty brine, so a good rinse with cold water prevents the finished dish from being too salty.

Frozen vegetables are another great option if the fresh versions are nowhere to be found. In many cases, frozen produce is of a higher quality than fresh, because it's picked at the peak of the season and flash frozen right in the field. Once defrosted, the texture can deteriorate, though. To avoid this, rinse frozen veggies in cold water and add to the dish as close to serving time as possible.

Artichoke Heart Salad

Garlic, oregano, and artichokes combine in this mouth-watering salad.

2 cloves garlic

$\frac{1}{2}$ tsp. dried oregano

$\frac{1}{2}$ tsp. fennel seed, crushed

$\frac{1}{4}$ cup orange juice

1 TB. olive oil

$\frac{1}{4}$ tsp. kosher salt

$\frac{1}{4}$ tsp. freshly ground black pepper

2 (14-oz.) cans artichoke hearts, drained

$\frac{1}{2}$ small red onion, sliced

1 pt. cherry tomatoes, halved

$\frac{1}{4}$ cup fresh basil or spinach leaves

2 TB. grated Parmesan cheese

Yield: 1 large salad
Prep time: 90 minutes
Serving size: $\frac{1}{4}$ salad

1. In a large bowl, whisk together garlic, oregano, fennel seed, orange juice, olive oil, kosher salt, and pepper.

2. Add drained artichoke hearts, onion, and tomatoes, and toss together to bend thoroughly. Cover and marinate in the refrigerator for 1 or 2 hours.

3. To serve, toss again to distribute dressing, add basil, and top with grated Parmesan cheese.

Variation: This salad is a great accompaniment to grilled meat and poultry. Or turn it into a meal by adding boiled and sliced new potatoes, grilled or canned tuna, and sliced black or kalamata olives.

 Salad Secret _____

Be sure to use plain canned artichoke hearts, not marinated. If you can't find them in a can, use an equivalent amount of frozen artichoke hearts. Marinated artichokes should be a last resort. They must be soaked and rinsed thoroughly.

Asian Slaw

Tangy and exotically spiced, this salad adds a refreshing twist to standard picnic fare.

1 clove garlic

1 TB. grated ginger root

1 TB. sesame oil

1 TB. soy sauce

½ cup rice vinegar

2 TB. peanut butter

4 cups napa cabbage, shredded

1 red bell pepper, ribs and seeds removed, and sliced thin

2 large carrots, grated

1 cup bean sprouts

4 scallions, chopped

¼ cup fresh cilantro leaves

1 TB. sesame seeds

¼ cup chopped cashews

Yield: 1 large salad
Prep time: 90 minutes
Serving size: ¼ salad

Tasty Morsel

Cilantro is a popular herb worldwide. It's common in Central American (such as Mexican) and South American cuisines, as well as most cuisines of Asia. You may know it as *Chinese parsley* or *fresh coriander*, so named because its dried seeds are the spice coriander.

1. In a large bowl, combine garlic, ginger root, sesame oil, soy sauce, rice vinegar, and peanut butter.

2. Add napa cabbage, red bell pepper, carrots, bean sprouts, and scallions, and toss to thoroughly coat. Cover and chill for 1 or 2 hours.

3. To serve, add cilantro, sesame seeds, and cashews, and toss again to distribute dressing.

Asparagus with Lemon Vinaigrette

This simple salad has a bright, fresh flavor that's a perfect complement to heavier foods like oily fish, rice, meats, or cream sauces.

1 lb. fresh asparagus

Zest and juice of 1 lemon

¼ tsp. kosher salt

¼ tsp. freshly ground black pepper

2 TB. olive oil

¼ cup chopped fresh parsley

Yield: 1 large salad
Prep time: 5 minutes
Cook time: 10 minutes
Serving size: ¼ salad

1. In a shallow sauté pan, bring 1 quart water to a boil over high heat. Add asparagus, and cook for 3 to 5 minutes or until bright green and tender (al dente). Drain and immediately plunge into ice water.

2. In a large bowl, whisk together lemon zest, lemon juice, kosher salt, pepper, and olive oil.

3. Add chilled asparagus, and toss to coat. Serve sprinkled with chopped parsley.

Salad Secret

This recipe is best in the springtime, when asparagus is young and tender. If you make it later in the year, when asparagus is thick and woody, peel the fibrous stems down to the tender centers. If no asparagus is available, try fresh green beans, wax beans, zucchini, or broccoli.

Caprese Salad

The green herby basil, white creamy cheese, and red sweet tomatoes of this sweet and creamy Italian salad are said to represent the colors of the Italian flag.

2 large, ripe tomatoes, sliced thinly

8 oz. buffalo mozzarella, sliced thinly

1 cup large fresh basil leaves

¼ cup extra-virgin olive oil

½ tsp. sea salt

½ tsp. freshly cracked black pepper

> **Yield: 4 small salads**
>
> **Prep time:** 20 minutes
>
> **Serving size:** 1 salad

1. On 4 serving plates, alternately arrange tomato slices, mozzarella slices, and basil leaves.

2. Drizzle with olive oil, sprinkle with sea salt and pepper, and serve.

Variation: For a towering presentation, layer the ingredients upright in a cylindrical mold or a soup can with the top and bottom removed.

Tasty Morsel

Mozzarella di Bufala Campana (the Italian name) is fresh (not aged) cheese made from the milk of water buffalos. It's exported to the United States and is also copied by several U.S. cheese manufacturers. Fresh mozzarella is sold floating in mild brine and should be consumed within 2 days of purchase. If you can't find fresh mozzarella, consider making another salad. There is nothing that compares.

Classic Coleslaw

This easy, crunchy, cabbage salad is a picnic classic. Add your own twist with black or golden raisins for a sweet, chewy surprise.

1 cup sour cream

1 tsp. celery seed

½ tsp. kosher salt

½ tsp. freshly ground black pepper

2 TB. lemon juice

1 medium white onion, grated

¼ cup fresh chives, chopped

½ head green cabbage, thinly shredded (about 2 cups)

½ head purple cabbage, thinly shredded (about 2 cups)

1 large carrot, grated

> **Yield: 1 large salad**
> **Prep time:** 20 minutes
> **Serving size:** ¼ salad

1. In a large bowl, stir together sour cream, celery seed, kosher salt, pepper, and lemon juice.

2. Add onion, chives, green cabbage, purple cabbage, and carrot, and toss to coat thoroughly. Serve chilled.

Tasty Morsel

The term *coleslaw* is probably an American corruption of the Dutch word *koolsla*, meaning "cabbage salad."

Creamy Summer Vegetable Salad

This cool, creamy salad highlights the bounty of summer and is best when made with a variety of fresh summer produce.

1 cup sour cream

Zest and juice of 1 lemon

1 tsp. dried thyme

¼ tsp. kosher salt

¼ tsp. freshly ground black pepper

½ cup chopped scallions

8 to 10 radishes, sliced

2 medium cucumbers, peeled, seeded, and sliced

3 medium tomatoes, sliced in wedges

Yield: 1 large salad
Prep time: 30 minutes, plus at least 1 hour to marinate
Serving size: ¼ salad

1. In a large bowl, stir together sour cream, lemon zest, lemon juice, thyme, kosher salt, and pepper.

2. Add scallions, radishes, cucumbers, and tomatoes, and toss well to coat.

3. Refrigerate for 1 or 2 hours before serving.

Variation: If your garden is overflowing with more vegetables than what's called for here, by all means, add it in.

Salad Secret

This salad is fine on its own, but try serving it in hollowed-out bell peppers, in bowls made of cabbage leaves, or rolled in tortillas for healthful wraps.

Cucumber-Mint Salad

This cool and refreshing salad is a perfect accompaniment to hot and spicy main dishes. You can turn it into traditional Greek tzatziki by adding dill, oregano, and parsley.

1 cup nonfat plain yogurt

1 tsp. ground cumin

¼ cup chopped fresh mint

½ tsp. kosher salt

2 medium cucumbers, peeled, seeded, and sliced

1 medium red onion, sliced

Yield: 1 large salad
Prep time: 20 minutes, plus at least 1 hour cooling time
Serving size: ¼ salad

1. In a large bowl, mix together yogurt, cumin, mint, and kosher salt.

2. Add cucumbers and onions, and toss to coat.

3. Refrigerate for 1 or 2 hours before serving.

Salad Secret

To seed a cucumber, peel it, slice it in half lengthwise, and remove the seeds by scraping out the center core with a spoon. Seeding a cucumber is purely aesthetic. Some people don't like the texture of the seeds, but the flavor is unremarkable and won't hurt if left in.

Greek Salad

This cool, cucumber salad is traditionally made without vinegar or lettuce. Fresh lemon juice, fruity olive oil, and salty feta create the perfect dressing.

4 large ripe tomatoes, sliced in wedges

2 medium cucumbers, peeled and sliced

1 small red onion, sliced thin

½ cup pitted kalamata olives

½ cup fresh flat Italian parsley leaves

1 TB. dried oregano

Juice of 1 lemon

¼ cup olive oil

¼ tsp. kosher salt

¼ tsp. freshly ground black pepper

1 cup feta cheese

> **Yield: 1 large salad**
>
> **Prep time:** 20 minutes
>
> **Serving size:** ¼ salad

1. In a large bowl, combine tomatoes, cucumbers, onion, olives, parsley, and oregano.

2. Add lemon juice, olive oil, kosher salt, pepper, and feta. Toss to coat, and serve.

Tasty Morsel _____

English cucumbers are interchangeable with standard cucumbers. They're longer, have fewer seeds, and cause fewer burps.

Radish and Onion Salad

This slightly spicy salad is great with grilled burgers or steaks. Or you can use it as a filling for finger sandwiches.

1 clove garlic

Juice of 1 lemon

2 TB. olive oil

1 tsp. honey

¼ cup fresh dill, minced

½ tsp. kosher salt

½ tsp. freshly ground black pepper

2 cups red radishes, sliced thin

2 cups cucumber, peeled, seeded, and sliced thin

1 small white onion, sliced thin

Yield: 1 large salad
Prep time: 30 minutes
Serving size: ¼ salad

1. In a large bowl, whisk together garlic, lemon juice, olive oil, honey, dill, kosher salt, and pepper.

2. Add radishes, cucumber, and onion. Toss to coat, and serve chilled.

Tasty Morsel

Red radishes are the norm, but they also come in other colors. Try white, pink, purple, spicy black, and the Asian diakon when you find them. You may also be familiar with their radish-y relations, horseradish and wasabi.

Sweet Pea Salad

This is a surprisingly refreshing salad. Some versions include sweet pickle relish, but here, the pineapple provides the sweet note.

1 lb. fresh shelled peas or 1 (16-oz.) pkg. frozen peas

¼ cup mayonnaise

¼ cup sour cream

1 TB. prepared horseradish

1 TB. Dijon mustard

½ small white onion, minced

¼ tsp. kosher salt

¼ tsp. freshly ground black pepper

2 stalks celery, chopped fine

1 (8-oz.) can crushed pineapple, drained

¼ cup fresh dill or parsley, chopped

Yield: 1 large salad
Prep time: 30 minutes
Serving size: ¼ salad

1. If using frozen peas, rinse them in a colander under cool water to defrost. Set aside to drain.

Salad Secret

Turn this salad into a meal by adding 2 cups cooked bay shrimp, crab, or imitation crab.

2. In a large bowl, whisk together mayonnaise, sour cream, horse-radish, and Dijon mustard. Add onion, kosher salt, pepper, celery, peas, and pineapple, and toss to coat.

3. Serve topped with chopped dill.

Chapter 5

Warm Salads

In This Chapter

- ◆ Warm, wilted leaves
- ◆ Roasted roots
- ◆ Beans and greens

What's the difference between a "side dish" and a "warm salad"? Is it all just in the name? To certain extent, yes. I mean, who's to tell me I can't call food what I want to at my own dinner table?

But believe it or not, there's a real distinction between the two. A "warm salad" is a warm dish with classic salad components. Any traditional salad with crisp, fresh veggies can be served warm. Greens can be heated on a grill or wilted with the addition of warm ingredients. Vegetables can be blanched or boiled and added to a dressing and served still warm. The dressing itself can also be warmed.

Adding warm elements can take your salad-making to a higher level. The most interesting dishes combine both hot and cold ingredients, which provides both textural and temperature contrasts.

Tips for Cooking Greens

When cooking greens, you must pay attention. It doesn't take long for greens to go from cooked to mushy. They should be warm, but still have a fresh, bright flavor.

Like all green vegetables, leaves will turn bright green as they cook and then change to a darker, dingier color. The key to wilted greens is to serve them at the perfect stage. Pull them off the heat in the brief moments when the color is the brightest, usually less than a minute into the heating process.

When the heating occurs with the addition of a hot dressing, there's no opportunity to stop the cooking, so serve warm salads immediately upon adding the warm dressing to keep the greens from over-cooking on the plate. To ease production, mix dressings ahead of time and heat at the last minute.

Grilled Romaine

The charcoal essence of this salad, mixed with its sweet, herby dressing, is a snap to make, especially when you've already got the grill on.

2 shallots, minced

1 tsp. herbes de Provence

1 TB. honey

¼ cup white wine vinegar

2 medium tomatoes, diced

½ cup olive oil

4 hearts of romaine

¼ tsp. kosher salt

¼ tsp. freshly ground black pepper

> **Yield: 4 hearts of romaine**
>
> **Prep time:** 10 minutes
>
> **Cook time:** 10 minutes
>
> **Serving size:** 1 heart of romaine

1. Preheat the grill to high.

2. In a small bowl, combine shallots, herbes de Provence, honey, white wine vinegar, tomatoes, and olive oil.

3. Brush romaine hearts with dressing, season with salt and pepper, and grill for 5 to 10 minutes, turning frequently, until charred.

4. Serve warm topped with diced tomatoes and drizzled with remaining dressing.

Salad Secret

Hearts of romaine are the inner leaves of the head of lettuce. You can purchase hearts, or you can simply strip the outer leaves off of a standard head. Be sure to save those outer leaves for another salad.

Old-Fashioned Wilted Green Salad

"Cooked greens" refers to a classic southern dish, usually consisting of collards or kale that's boiled for hours with pork. This garlicky and sweet version is fresher and more modern. It's not quite as time-consuming, and it's quite a bit more healthful.

¼ cup olive oil

1 medium red onion, diced

2 cloves garlic, minced

1 bunch *Swiss chard*, washed and trimmed

1 bunch mustard greens, washed and trimmed

1 bunch spinach, washed and trimmed

¼ tsp. kosher salt

¼ tsp. freshly ground black pepper

Zest and juice of 1 orange

Yield: 1 large salad
Prep time: 15 minutes
Cook time: 10 minutes
Serving size: ¼ salad

1. In a large sauté pan over high heat, heat olive oil. Add onion and cook until translucent. Add garlic and cook until golden.

2. Reduce heat to medium, and add Swiss chard, mustard greens, and spinach all at once. Toss with tongs, and season with salt and pepper.

3. When bright green and slightly wilted, add orange zest and orange juice, toss to coat, and serve immediately.

 Lettuce Lingo

Swiss chard, or *chard, mangold,* and *silverbeet,* is a big green leaf, fairly thick, with firm white, yellow, or red veins. It's the same species as the beet, although it's grown for its leaves, not its root.

Spinach Salad with Warm Bacon Dressing

This is the epitome of a warm salad. Hot, crisp, tangy, salty, and sweet, it's a classic.

2 bunches spinach, washed and trimmed

6 slices uncooked bacon, diced

2 cloves garlic

2 TB. Dijon mustard

2 TB. cider vinegar

2 TB. honey

Salt and pepper

1 cup sourdough croutons

Yield: 1 large salad
Prep time: 10 minutes
Cook time: 10 minutes
Serving size: ¼ salad

1. Place washed spinach in a large salad bowl, and set aside.

2. In a small sautée pan over high heat, sauté bacon for 2 or 3 minutes or until fat is rendered. Add garlic, and continue to cook for another 1 or 2 until bacon is crisp. Remove from heat, and drain off all but 3 tablespoons bacon drippings.

3. Add Dijon mustard, cider vinegar, honey, salt, and pepper to bacon. Whisk thoroughly and drizzle over spinach. Toss and serve immediately, topped with sourdough croutons.

Lettuce Lingo

The term *rendered* here refers to using heat to melt the fat out of a fatty food. Any animal fat can be rendered, and the fat can then be used for cooking in lieu of oil or butter. Lard is rendered pork fat, schmaltz is rendered chicken fat, and duck confit is a dish traditionally cooked and preserved in rendered duck fat.

Warm Beet and Berry Salad

Roasted beets are sweet, juicy, and gorgeous. They're also loaded with nutrients, including folic acid, and antioxidants.

5 large beets, scrubbed

¼ cup olive oil

1 medium red onion

2 TB. balsamic vinegar

1 TB. fresh thyme, chopped

1 TB. fresh oregano, chopped

2 TB. fresh grated or prepared horseradish

2 cloves garlic, minced

½ cup raspberries

½ cup fresh or frozen blackberries, thawed if frozen

4 cups fresh spinach leaves, shredded

¼ cup dried cranberries

¼ cup sliced almonds

Yield: 1 large salad
Prep time: 20 minutes
Cook time: 1 hour
Serving size: ¼ salad

1. Preheat the oven to 450°F.

2. Coat beets lightly in 1 tablespoon olive oil, and wrap together in a large piece of foil. Bake for about 1 hour or until tender to the touch. Cool until they can be handled, peel, and slice thinly.

3. While beets are baking, chop and soak onion in cold water for 15 to 30 minutes. Drain and set aside.

> **Heads-Up!**
> Consider wearing gloves while peeling and slicing beets. You may also want an apron

4. In a large bowl, whisk together balsamic vinegar, thyme, oregano, horseradish, garlic, raspberries, and blackberries. Drizzle in remaining olive oil while whisking.

5. Add beets, onion, and spinach, and toss to coat. Serve warm topped with cranberries and almonds.

Warm Brussels Sprout Salad

One taste of this warm, buttery salad, and you'll never turn your nose up at brussels sprouts again.

4 cups brussels sprouts

4 TB. unsalted butter

1 shallot, minced

1 clove garlic, minced

1 TB. fresh thyme leaves, minced

¼ cup tarragon vinegar

¼ cup shaved Parmesan cheese

Yield: 1 large salad
Prep time: 10 minutes
Cook time: 20 minutes
Serving size: ¼ salad

1. In a large saucepan over high heat, bring 2 quarts water to a boil. Add brussels sprouts, and cook for about 2 or 3 minutes or until bright green. Drain immediately and submerge in ice water to stop the cooking. Remove leaves and set aside.

2. In a large sauté pan over medium heat, melt butter. Add shallot and garlic, and cook for 2 or 3 minutes or until golden. Add brussels sprout leaves, and cook for 1 or 2 minutes, tossing to coat.

3. Remove from heat, and add thyme and tarragon vinegar. Toss to coat, and serve immediately, topped with Parmesan cheese.

 Salad Secret

To remove leaves from the tight brussels sprout heads, use a small sharp knife to trim off the stem end. Pull off a layer of leaves, and trim again. Continue pulling and trimming until you're left with only the center core. Cut the core in half and use it in the recipe, too.

Warm German Potato Salad

This salad is tangy from the cider vinegar, salty from the bacon, and a classic because it's so delicious!

2 lb. red new potatoes (about 6 to 8 small)

6 slices uncooked bacon, diced

1 medium yellow onion, chopped

1 cup celery, chopped

2 cloves garlic, minced

1 tsp. dill seed

1 TB. sugar

½ cup cider vinegar

2 TB. seeded spicy mustard

¼ tsp. kosher salt

¼ tsp. freshly ground black pepper

Yield: 1 large salad
Prep time: 30 minutes
Cook time: 15 minutes
Serving size: ¼ salad

1. In a large saucepan, add potatoes and cover with cold water. Set over high heat, and bring to a boil. Reduce heat to medium, and simmer for about 20 minutes or until potatoes are tender. Drain potatoes and submerge in a bowl of ice water until cool. Peel, slice, and set aside.

2. In a large sauté pan over medium heat, cook bacon for 2 or 3 minutes or until crisp. Remove bacon from the pan, add onion and celery, and cook for about 5 minutes or until translucent.

3. Add garlic, dill seed, sugar, cider vinegar, spicy mustard, and sliced potatoes. Cook gently for 2 or 3 minutes or until all ingredients are warmed. Add bacon, season with kosher salt and pepper, and serve warm.

 Heads-Up!

Don't use mealy baking potatoes for this recipe; they'll disintegrate into mashed potatoes, which may taste good, but definitely can't be called a warm salad. Use waxy new potatoes instead.

Warm Pumpkin and Bacon Salad

This salty, tangy, crunchy, and creamy recipe is the most sophisticated potato salad in town. The combination of flavors and textures makes it fit for your most elegant meal.

1 medium pumpkin or 1 large butternut squash

2 TB. olive oil

¼ tsp. kosher salt

¼ tsp. freshly ground black pepper

4 slices uncooked bacon, diced

4 scallions, minced

1 clove garlic, minced

½ cup chopped pecans

¼ tsp. ground nutmeg

Zest and juice of 1 orange

¼ cup goat cheese, crumbled

> **Yield: 1 large salad**
>
> **Prep time:** 15 minutes
>
> **Cook time:** 30 minutes
>
> **Serving size:** ¼ salad

1. Preheat the oven to 450°F.

2. Peel, seed, and dice pumpkin into 2-inch cubes. Toss pumpkin with olive oil, and spread in a single layer on a baking sheet. Sprinkle with kosher salt, and pepper, and roast for about 20 minutes or until tender and browned. Toss occasionally for even cooking.

3. Meanwhile, in a large sauté pan over medium heat, cook bacon for 2 or 3 minutes or until fat is rendered.

4. Add scallions, garlic, and pecans, and cook for 2 or 3 minutes or until golden and toasted. Remove from heat, and stir in nutmeg, orange zest, and orange juice. Set aside.

5. Combine warm pumpkin and dressing, and toss thoroughly. Serve immediately, topped with crumbled goat cheese.

Tasty Morsel

Good pumpkins are only around for a short time in the fall, but you can usually find butternut squash in the supermarket. You can try this recipe with other winter squash, too, like acorn, kabocha, Hubbard, or turban, to name a few.

Warm Red Cabbage Salad

Sweet apples and onions pair with tangy cider vinegar for a crunchy, sweet, and sour salad. It's a perfect side dish for fatty meats, like pot roast or salmon.

4 TB. olive oil

1 clove garlic

1 medium red onion, sliced thin

1 small head purple cabbage, shredded

$\frac{1}{4}$ tsp. kosher salt

$\frac{1}{4}$ tsp. ground pepper

1 fuji apple, peeled and grated

3 TB. cider vinegar

1 TB. fresh Italian parsley, chopped

1 TB. fresh oregano, chopped

Yield: 1 large salad
Prep time: 15 minutes
Cook time: 10 minutes
Serving size: $\frac{1}{4}$ salad

1. In a large sauté pan over high heat, heat olive oil. Add garlic and onion, and cook for 2 or 3 minutes or until tender.

2. Add cabbage, kosher salt, pepper, and cook, tossing, for about 3 to 5 minutes or until wilted.

3. Remove from heat, add apple, cider vinegar, parsley, and oregano, and toss to coat. Serve immediately.

Tasty Morsel _____

Purple cabbage is the same thing as red cabbage. The pigment is caused by anthocyanin pigment molecules, which are altered by the pH levels in their environment. In the garden, acidic soil turns the cabbage red, while an alkaline soil makes it blue. In a recipe, the addition of acid (such as the vinegar here) also turns the cabbage red.

Winter Bean Salad

Tangy, sun-dried tomatoes and Parmesan cheese lend a distinctive Italian flavor to these tender beans.

3 TB. olive oil

1 medium red onion, diced

2 stalks celery, diced

1 large carrot, grated

2 cloves garlic, minced

¼ cup oil-packed sun-dried tomatoes, chopped

2 TB. fresh rosemary, minced

½ cup red wine vinegar

1 (15-oz.) can white cannellini beans, drained and rinsed

1 (15-oz.) can lima beans, drained and rinsed

1 (15-oz.) can kidney beans, drained and rinsed

¼ cup shredded Parmesan cheese

> **Yield: 1 large salad**
>
> **Prep time:** 10 minutes
>
> **Cook time:** 15 minutes
>
> **Serving size:** ¼ salad

1. Heat olive oil in a large sauté pan over medium heat. Add onion and celery, and cook for 2 or 3 minutes or until translucent.

2. Add carrot and garlic, and cook for 2 or 3 minutes or until garlic turns golden. Stir in sun-dried tomatoes, rosemary, and red wine vinegar, and remove from heat.

3. In a large salad bowl, combine cannellini beans, lima beans, kidney beans, and dressing, and toss thoroughly. Serve immediately, topped with Parmesan cheese.

Salad Secret

Sun-dried tomatoes are available both marinated and dry. Marinated is best for this recipe, but if you have trouble locating them, you can soak dried tomatoes in warm water for 10 to 15 minutes before using. The dressing is flavorful enough that you won't be able to tell the difference.

Chapter 6

Potato Salads

In This Chapter

- ◆ Classic spuds
- ◆ Flavorful dressings
- ◆ Interesting combinations

Potato salad is one of America's favorites. Recipes are passed from generation to generation and served with pride at picnics from coast to coast. In this chapter, you'll find some basics as well as some unique variations to spice up your next family reunion.

Potato Varieties

The most important ingredient in a potato salad is, of course, the potato. For most of the recipes in this chapter, you want firm chunks of potatoes, not a mealy mash. To achieve this, choose a potato with low starch, or waxy potatoes.

Waxy potatoes, also known as boiling potatoes, are distinguished by their thin skins and low starch content, which helps them hold their shape when cooked. Waxy potatoes include the new potato; red-, yellow-, gold-, white-, and purple-skinned potatoes; as well as the heirloom-variety fingerlings. Baker, russet, Idaho, and Burbank potatoes are all mealy and more suited to baked potatoes and french fries than potato salad.

Neither kind of potatoes should be refrigerated. Low temperatures convert some of their starch to sugar, which can alter recipes, especially when direct heat is applied. A potato with excess sugar can burn easily. Store them out of direct sunlight, in a cool, dry spot.

Boiling Potatoes

In most cases, the potatoes in these recipes are boiled whole. The finished shape of the potato will be more uniform if you wait to cut it after cooking, and there's less chance of overcooking. In addition, all vegetables leach their nutrients into the cooking liquid, so the less surface area that's exposed, the fewer nutrients that are lost.

Boil potatoes by covering them with at least 1 inch of cold water. They should be submerged to allow for evaporation, and the water should initially be cold to help keep the cooking temperature even. Regardless of what the recipe says (here or in other books), it's a good idea to check for doneness a bit sooner than the recommended time. Pot, water level, potato size, stove efficiency, and even altitude all play a part in cooking time. Test for doneness by gently inserting a knife. It should slide in easily and not break the potato apart.

Dressing Safety

One of the most common foodborne illness disasters is caused by potato salad. Potato salad mixed with mayonnaise, that is.

Mayonnaise is an egg-based dressing and, therefore, it's a source of moist protein. Moist protein is bacteria's favorite breeding ground, especially when warm. Food service professionals know that the danger zone for bacteria breeding is between 41°F and 145°F. That means that just out of the fridge, or just out of the oven, are fine. But protein foods that sit in the trunk of your car while you drive an hour to your favorite picnic spot are not recommended.

To prevent foodborne illness at your next picnic, use a cooler. Better yet, serve a vinaigrette-based dressing instead of a mayonnaise-based one.

Classic Potato Salad

The Dijon mustard and onion give this classic salad a subtle kick.

2 lb. red new potatoes (about 6 to 8 small potatoes)

1½ cups mayonnaise

2 TB. Dijon mustard

¼ cup cider or vinegar

½ tsp. grated nutmeg

¼ tsp. kosher salt

¼ tsp. freshly ground black pepper

1 cup celery, chopped

1 cup yellow onion, chopped

Yield: 1 large salad

Prep time: 20 minutes

Cook time: 30 minutes

Serving size: ¼ salad

1. In a large saucepan, cover potatoes with cold water and bring to a boil over high heat. Reduce heat to medium, and simmer for about 20 minutes or until potatoes are tender. Drain and submerge potatoes in ice water until cool. Cut into quarters and set aside.

2. In a large bowl, whisk together mayonnaise, Dijon mustard, cider, nutmeg, kosher salt, and pepper.

3. Add potatoes, celery, onion, and toss to coat. Chill at least 1 hour before serving.

Salad Secret

This is the simple classic, but you can personalize it to your heart's content. Lots of folks like to add sweet pickles or relish, green onions, bell peppers, or radishes.

Cheesy Potato Salad

Sharp cheddar, the sharper the better, is a natural with potatoes. Here, creamy cream cheese adds an additional tang.

2 lb. red new potatoes (about 6 to 8 small potatoes)

½ cup sour cream

1 (8-oz.) pkg. cream cheese, softened

2 TB. honey

2 TB. white wine vinegar

1 cup sharp *cheddar cheese*, grated

¼ tsp. kosher salt

¼ tsp. freshly ground black pepper

1 cup bacon, cooked crisp and crumbled

¼ cup fresh chives, chopped

Yield: 1 large salad
Prep time: 40 minutes
Cook time: 30 minutes
Serving size: ¼ salad

1. In a large saucepan, cover potatoes with cold water and bring to a boil over high heat. Reduce heat to medium, and simmer for about 20 minutes or until potatoes are tender. Drain and submerge potatoes in ice water until cool. Cut into quarters and set aside.

2. In a large bowl, combine sour cream, cream cheese, honey, and white wine vinegar.

3. Stir in cheddar cheese, salt, pepper, bacon, and potatoes. Chill and serve, topped with chives.

Lettuce Lingo

Cheddar cheese is English in origin, from the village of Cheddar in Somerset in the fifteenth century. Today it's produced around the world. For a truly special salad, try some of the more interesting cheddars, such as coon cheddar from New York, sharp white Vermont cheddar, Texas longhorn, or Oregon Tillamook.

Curry Potato Salad

This exotic-flavored salad is mild in the world of curry but is a nice intro-
duction to the curry novice. Pair it with exotic roast meats or stews.

2 lb. red new potatoes (about 6 to 8 small
potatoes)

1 cup yogurt

1 cup mayonnaise

1 TB. rice vinegar

2 TB. curry powder or paste

¼ tsp. kosher salt

¼ tsp. freshly ground black pepper

2 stalks celery, chopped

3 scallions, chopped

2 fuji apples (or your choice), grated

½ cup black or golden raisins

1 cup sliced almonds, toasted

Yield: 1 large salad
Prep time: 20 minutes
Cook time: 20 minutes
Serving size: ¼ salad

1. In a large saucepan, cover potatoes with cold water and bring to a
   boil over high heat. Reduce heat to medium, and simmer for about
   20 minutes or potatoes are until tender. Drain and submerge potatoes
   in ice water until cool. Cut into quarters and set aside.

2. In a large bowl, whisk together yogurt, mayonnaise, rice vinegar,
   curry powder, kosher salt, and pepper.

3. Stir in celery, scallions, apples, raisins, and potatoes, and mix thoroughly. Chill and serve topped with almonds.

Tasty Morsel

Each region of India has its typical curry spice blends, and each
cook within that region has his or her own interpretation of those
blends. What's more, Indian spices are rarely pre-mixed in India
like they are here.

Dilly Potato Salad

Dill greens, flowers, and seeds are commonly paired with fish, so this salad is the perfect accompaniment to all your favorite seafood meals.

2 lb. red new potatoes (about 6 to 8 small potatoes)

1 cup mayonnaise

2 TB. Dijon mustard

Zest and juice of 1 lemon

1/4 cup fresh dill, minced

1/2 tsp. dill seed, crushed

1 shallot, minced

3 stalks celery, chopped

5 or 6 radishes, chopped

1/4 tsp. kosher salt

1/4 tsp. freshly ground black pepper

Yield: 1 large salad
Prep time: 20 minutes
Cook time: 30 minutes
Serving size: 1/4 salad

1. In a large saucepan, cover potatoes with cold water and bring to a boil over high heat. Reduce heat to medium, and simmer for about 20 minutes or until potatoes are tender. Drain and submerge potatoes in ice water until cool. Cut into quarters and set aside.

2. In a large bowl, whisk together mayonnaise, Dijon mustard, lemon zest, and lemon juice.

3. Stir in potatoes, fresh dill, dill seed, shallot, celery, radishes, kosher salt, and pepper. Chill before serving.

Tasty Morsel

The fine, threadlike dill leaves have been used since the Middle Ages as an herbal remedy to relieve upset stomachs and protect against witchcraft. The aroma of all parts resembles caraway and anise, but has a more sour, vinegary essence. Dill, dill seed, and dried dill weed are readily available in most markets.

Apple and Potato Salad

Crunchy and fresh apples and celery make this a more substantial version of the Waldorf. Serve it with your favorite sandwich.

2 lb. red new potatoes (about 6 to 8 small potatoes)

½ cup sour cream

½ cup mayonnaise

¼ cup apple juice

1 red apple, diced

1 green apple, diced

3 stalks celery

¼ cup fresh chives, chopped

¼ tsp. kosher salt

¼ tsp. freshly ground black pepper

½ cup walnuts, toasted and chopped

Yield: 1 large salad
Prep time: 20 minutes
Cook time: 30 minutes
Serving size: ¼ salad

1. In a large saucepan, cover potatoes with cold water and bring to a boil over high heat. Reduce heat to medium, and simmer for about 20 minutes or until potatoes are tender. Drain and submerge potatoes in ice water until cool. Cut into quarters and set aside.

2. In a large bowl, whisk together sour cream, mayonnaise, and apple juice.

3. Toss in potatoes, red apple, green apple, celery, chives, kosher salt, and pepper, and mix thoroughly. Chill and serve topped with walnuts.

Heads-Up!

Apples begin oxidizing, or turning brown, as soon as you cut them. Chefs have long soaked them in acidulated water (water with acid, usually lemon juice) to slow the process, but apples hold water, which when released can thin out your salad dressing. Unless you have to make the recipe far in advance, add the apples at the last minute.

New Potato Vinaigrette

This recipe highlights the simple flavor of the potato, often hidden by creamy dressings of other potato salads. It's a fresh and pure salute to the spud.

2 lb. yellow new potatoes (about 6 to 8 small potatoes)

3 TB. olive oil

3 TB. balsamic vinegar

1 TB. Dijon mustard

¼ cup fresh *chervil*

¼ tsp. kosher salt

¼ tsp. freshly ground black pepper

> **Yield: 1 large salad**
>
> **Prep time:** 40 minutes
>
> **Cook time:** 10 minutes plus 60 minutes to chill
>
> **Serving size:** ¼ salad

1. In a large saucepan, cover potatoes with cold water and bring to a boil over high heat. Reduce heat to medium, and simmer for about 20 minutes or until potatoes are tender. Drain and submerge potatoes in ice water until cool. Cut into thin wheel slices and set aside.

2. In a large bowl, whisk together olive oil, balsamic vinegar, Dijon mustard, chervil, kosher salt, and pepper.

3. Add sliced potatoes, and toss thoroughly. Chill before serving.

Lettuce Lingo

Chervil is an indispensable element of French cuisine and a crucial ingredient in the classic herb blends *fines herbes* and *herbes de Provence*. Its fine, lacy leaves and delicate white flowers have a slight anise flavor, which complements all sorts of foods, including fish, poultry, eggs, cheese, soups, and salads.

Red Potato Salad with Stilton

Some consider Stilton the king of cheese. It certainly has a regal flavor. Its salty tang pairs beautifully with sweet dried figs.

2 lb. red new potatoes (about 6 to 8 small potatoes)

½ cup mayonnaise

½ cup Stilton cheese, crumbled

3 scallions, chopped

3 stalks celery, chopped

¼ tsp. kosher salt

¼ tsp. freshly ground black pepper

¼ tsp. ground fennel seed

¼ cup walnut halves, toasted

¼ cup dried black figs, diced

Yield: 1 large salad
Prep time: 20 minutes
Cook time: 30 minutes
Serving size: ¼ salad

1. In a large saucepan, cover potatoes with cold water and bring to a boil over high heat. Reduce heat to medium, and simmer for about 20 minutes or until potatoes are tender. Drain and submerge potatoes in ice water until cool. Dice and set aside.

2. In a large bowl, whisk together mayonnaise, Stilton, scallions, celery, salt, pepper, and fennel seed.

3. Add potatoes, walnuts, and figs, and toss to coat. Chill before serving.

Variation: If you can't find Stilton, you can replace it with a more humble blue cheese.

 Tasty Morsel _____

Botanically, figs are not one fruit. What we think of as the fig seeds are really hundreds of tiny male and female fruits growing together inside a vase-shape skin called a *syconium*.

Scandinavian Potato Salad

The magic of this salad is in the dill and pickled herring. Sweet and creamy, it's a meal in itself. You can try it with smoked salmon, too.

2 lb. red new potatoes (about 6 to 8 small potatoes)

1½ cups sour cream

½ cup fresh dill, chopped

¼ tsp. ground caraway seed

¼ tsp. kosher salt

½ large red onion, sliced thin

1 cup chopped pickled herring

Yield: 1 large salad
Prep time: 20 minutes
Cook time: 30 minutes
Serving size: ¼ salad

1. In a large saucepan, cover potatoes with cold water and bring to a boil over high heat. Reduce heat to medium, and simmer for about 20 minutes or until potatoes are tender. Drain and submerge potatoes in ice water until cool. Cut into quarters and set aside.

2. In a large bowl, whisk together sour cream, dill, caraway seed, and kosher salt.

3. Add potatoes, onion, and pickled herring, and toss together thoroughly. Chill before serving.

 Tasty Morsel _____

Pickled herring is first cured in salt and then cured in a vinegar brine. Besides being a Scandinavian treat, similar recipes are found in Dutch, Japanese, and Ashkenazi Jewish cuisines

Sweet Potato and Pecan Salad

Sweet, creamy, and crunchy, this salad is perfect alongside leftover Thanksgiving turkey sandwiches.

2 lb. sweet potatoes (about 3 to 5 small potatoes)

3 TB. olive oil

1 clove garlic, minced

2 shallots, minced

2 TB. maple syrup

2 TB. cider vinegar

½ cup whole pecans, toasted

Yield: 1 large salad
Prep time: 20 minutes
Cook time: 30 minutes
Serving size: ¼ salad

1. Preheat the oven to 450°F.

2. Coat sweet potatoes lightly in 1 tablespoon olive oil, and wrap together in a large piece of aluminum foil. Bake for about 1 hour or until tender to the touch. Cool, peel, and slice thinly.

3. In a large bowl, whisk together garlic, shallots, maple syrup, cider vinegar, and remaining 2 tablespoons olive oil. Add sweet potatoes and pecans, and toss to coat. Chill and serve.

Tasty Morsel _____

Yams or sweet potatoes? They're similar but two different plant species. Many people and even markets get the two confused. Canned yams are frequently sweet potatoes.) The sweet potato is the nutritional powerhouse, outperforming all other vegetables with vitamins A and C, iron, calcium, and fiber. Eating 1 sweet potato with its skin gives you more fiber than a bowl of oatmeal.

Chapter 7

Fruit Salads

In This Chapter

- ◆ Fruit facts
- ◆ Sweet and tangy fruit dressings
- ◆ Fresh and fruity combinations

Fruit salads are really more breakfast or dessert food than dinner fare, but no one will fault you if you spoon up a healthy helping of Ambrosia with your burger.

Choosing the Best Fruits

We're lucky to live in an age when fruits and vegetables are transported around the globe on a daily basis. If it's not ripe in your neck of the woods, chances are it's ripe somewhere else and is sitting in your local produce section. That does not mean, however, that the fruit is at the ideal stage of ripeness.

Whenever possible, choose fruit that's local and in season. Seasons vary by region, but for the most part, juicy stone fruits and berries are available in the warm months, while apples, pears, and citrus come in cooler months. Check your area for local farms and farmers' markets to make the most of your local products. Locally grown foods taste better, are fresher, and impact the environment less. (Flying in blueberries from Chile leaves a gigantic carbon footprint!)

Citrus Fruits

Citrus is valued not only for its fruit and juice, but for the aroma of its peel, too. The essential oils in the peel add their aroma to foods of all kinds. It can be used fresh, grated, peeled from the fruit, chopped fine, infused in chunks, or dried and pulverized to a powder.

Winter is the best season for citrus. It is then that you can find all sorts of fanciful varieties, including mandarins, tangerines, kumquats, blood oranges, and ruby red grapefruits.

Lemons

Lemons are used in many of this book's recipes, especially for their zest and juice. About 50 lemon varieties are cultivated throughout the Mediterranean, Greece, Spain, Italy, and North Africa. The majority of lemons, however, are grown in California. More lemons are grown in California than in all of Europe combined.

The Eureka and Lisbon varieties are the most common kinds of lemon.

Limes

Limes are in the same botanical family as lemons. They were originally introduced to Europe from Persia during the crusades and were highly prized for their oil-rich zest and floral aroma. Because the lime is high in vitamin C, British sailors were given a daily ration of lime to prevent scurvy, which is where the nickname *Limey*, meaning "Brit," originated.

The most common variety is the green Persian lime. The key, or Mexican, lime is sporadically available, especially in winter. They are much smaller and much more fragrant and ripen from green to yellow.

Oranges

The common sweet orange is probably a hybrid of ancient pomelos and tangerines that grew wild throughout Asia. They were brought to the new world both by Juan Ponce de Leon and Christopher Columbus. Several varieties and hybrids exist today, including the bitter Seville, the sweet Valencia, and the navel. The blood orange, grown throughout the Mediterranean and more recently in California, contains streaks of red pigment on its skin and within it.

Tasty Morsel

Rumor has it, the blood orange was cross-pollinated with a rose.

The mandarin is a small, sweet orange with loose skin. The tangerine is less sweet, and the tangelo is hybrid of tangerine and pomelo. The pomelo, also known as the shaddock, is the largest and oldest citrus fruit, native to Southeast Asia. It tastes like a sweet, mild grapefruit and has a very thick peel.

The grapefruit is hybrid of pomelo and orange and is named for the way the fruit clusters on the branch.

Tropical Fruits

You can find and enjoy a number of tropical fruits, but the most common ones found in American grocery stores include the banana, pineapple, mango, papaya, and kiwi.

Bananas

Bananas are full of starch, which converts to sugar quickly at room temperature. They grow on what looks like a tree, but is actually a large, perennial flowering herb. The leaves and flowers are added into stews, soups, used as wrapping for steamed and grilled foods, and often serve as a plate.

Bananas are an important food source in tropical nations and come in many varieties, including those that ripen to yellow, purple, black, and red. The most commonly eaten banana in the United States is the sweet dessert banana, known as the Cavendish. It ripens yellow and is best eaten when its skin is yellow with speckles of brown. Similar varieties include the short and chunky Burro and the dainty finger bananas.

Plantains are not as sweet when ripe and are used as a starch food in much of the world, as we would use potatoes.

Bananas oxidize when cut, just like apples and pears, and can be acidulated in the same manner to slow the effect (see the "Apples and Pears" section earlier in this chapter).

Pineapples

The pineapple is grown extensively in Central America and Hawaii. Pineapple is readily available canned, but nothing beats a fresh, ripe pineapple. Look for yellow, fragrant skin, and avoid pineapples with brown or mushy spots.

> **Heads-Up!**
> Eating too much pineapple irritates the mouth because the fruit contains the enzyme *bromaline*, a natural meat tenderizer. This enzyme breaks down protein and is the reason fresh pineapple added to gelatin prevents it from setting. Heat neutralizes this enzyme, though, so canned pineapple, which is heated when canned, is less irritable and can be used in your favorite Jell-O salad.

To access the sweet fruit of the pineapple, first cut the top and bottom off so it sits steadily on the counter. Then, using a sharp serrated knife, trim off the skin, working from top to bottom. Quarter the fruit, and remove the core, which is too fibrous to serve but makes a good snack. Cut as needed, and store unused pineapple in the fridge for up to a week, or freeze for a month.

Mangoes

Mangoes are popular around the world and were probably first grown in India as early as 3000 B.C.E. The fruit is common in cuisines of the East, Middle East, and Pacific and can be seen used in several forms, including ripe, green (unripe), dried, and powdered.

The fruit inside is orange, juicy, and somewhat fibrous, clinging firm to the skin and pit. The easiest way to liberate the fruit is to cut along either side of the oblong pit with a sharp knife to produce two halves. Then, with a large metal spoon, scoop the fruit out of the skin and cut as desired. The small amount of fruit left around the pit can be trimmed away.

The most common mango varieties in the United Stated are the Tommy Atkins, Haden, and Kent, which ripen from green to red/orange. The smaller yellow Ataulfo from Hawaii and Indonesia is bright yellow when ripe and very sweet with comparatively little fiber.

Papayas

Papayas come in two distinctively different varieties. Hawaiian papayas ripen to yellow and are small—about the size of a softball. Mexican papayas, which ripen to an orange/pink color, are much larger and can grow as big as a football or bigger. The flavors are similar and can be used interchangeably.

Tasty Morsel _____

Some cultures dry and grind the papaya seed and use it to season food, much like pepper

Papaya skin is thin and easy to remove with a peeler. Once peeled, cut the fruit in half and scoop out the tiny black seeds with a spoon.

Kiwi Fruit

The kiwi is a native of New Zealand and took on the name only after its export failed under the name Chinese gooseberry. Since the 1970s, it has become a wildly popular fruit in the United States, both for its bright exotic color and its high vitamin C content. More than 50 varieties of kiwi are grown worldwide, but the most common sold in the market is the Hayward.

The fuzzy skin is edible, but some cooks prefer to remove it. You can do this easily with the help of a trusty spoon. Slice off the top and bottom, and slide an ordinary spoon between the fruit and the skin, right next to the skin. Ease the spoon in until it comes out the other cut end, and gently rotate the kiwi to loosen the entire skin. The naked kiwi will slip right out and can then be cut into wheels, wedges, or chunks to suit your recipe.

Stone Fruits

Peaches, plums, apricots, and cherries are all considered stone fruits because they have stones, or pits, in the center. The larger stone fruits need not be peeled because the skins are thin and not offensive to the palate.

You can eat the fuzzy peach skin. If you want to remove it, it must be removed by blanching and shocking because the skin is too thin, and the fruit too juicy, to use a peeler. Score an X at the base of the ripened fruit, drop it in boiling water for 30 seconds, and immediately transfer it to ice water. When cool, the skin will slide right off.

Peaches

Peaches probably originated in China and made their way to Persia along the Silk Road. The peach, and its fuzz-free cousin the nectarine, come either freestone or clingstone, which means the pit either sticks to the fruit or drops out easily.

There are sweet white varieties, as well as more acidic yellow-flesh varieties of both nectarines and peaches. Both can have red/orange skin when ripe.

Plums

The ancient Romans, Japanese, and Chinese all knew the plum, and its use varied from fresh and dried fruit, to wine making, and medicinal use of the pit.

Thousands of varieties are available worldwide and more than 100 are available in the United States, mainly in the summer months. Colors include red, purple, green, yellow, amber, black, pink, and variegated. Most common are the Damson, Greengage, Satsuma, Golden, and Mirabelle.

Dried plums, or prunes, are also popular. (Don't get tricked into paying more for dried plums. They're still prunes.)

Apricots

The Armenians popularized the apricot, which is originally from China. It was brought to California in the late 1700s, where it thrived in the Mediterranean-like climate.

Ripe in the summer, fresh apricots should be orange and slightly soft. Dried apricots are a winter treat and should be soft and not too leathery.

Cherries

Cherries are thought to have originated in Persia and were known in ancient Rome. The two main varieties grown for consumption are the sweet and sour cherry. Within each category are several cultivars. Common sweet cherries include the Bing, Rainier, Royal Anne. Sour varieties include the Nanking and Evans.

Cherries must be pitted, a job that can be done by hand (wear gloves) or with any number of cherry-pitting tools available. Pitted cherries will keep for several months in the freezer.

Waldorf Salad

This classic crunchy, sweet luncheon salad is a perfectly fruity accompaniment to burgers and sandwiches.

2 red apples, diced, skin on

4 stalks celery, diced

1 cup walnuts, toasted and chopped

1 cup green or red grapes, halved

1 cup mayonnaise

Yield: 1 large salad
Prep time: 15 minutes
Serving size: ¼ salad

1. In a large bowl, combine apples, celery, walnuts, and grapes.

2. Toss with mayonnaise to coat, and serve chilled.

Tasty Morsel

Named for the super-deluxe Waldorf Astoria Hotel in New York City, this salad was not the brainstorm of the chef, but the maître d'hôtel, Oscar Tschirky. The original version dated to the 1890s used only apples, celery, and mayonnaise. Nuts and grapes began appearing in recipes in the 1920s.

Almond and Mandarin Salad

Napa cabbage and bok choy give this salad a refreshing crunch. Soy sauce, rice vinegar, and cilantro create an Asian flavor.

2 TB. peanut oil

2 TB. rice vinegar

1 TB. honey

1 TB. soy sauce

1 to 3 tsp. hot pepper sauce

½ head napa cabbage, shredded (about 2 cups)

1 large bok choy, shredded (about 2 cups)

2 scallions, sliced thin on an angle

½ cup sliced almonds

1 large carrot, grated

1 (10-oz.) can mandarin segments, rinsed and drained

¼ cup fresh cilantro leaves

> **Yield: 1 large salad**
> **Prep time:** 30 minutes
> **Serving size:** ¼ salad

1. In a large bowl, whisk together peanut oil, rice vinegar, honey, soy sauce, and hot pepper sauce.

2. Add cabbage, bok choy, scallions, almonds, carrot, mandarin segments, and cilantro, and toss thoroughly.

3. Set aside for 10 to 15 minutes before serving to allow the flavors to intensify.

Salad Secret _____

If you make this salad in the winter, use fresh mandarins or tangy tangerines. But if it looks good to you in the summer, go ahead and buy your mandarins in a can. They're often packed in sugar syrup, so be sure to rinse and drain them before using.

Ambrosia

This sweet, tropical salad is sure to please the young at your table as well as the young at heart.

1 (3-oz.) pkg. orange gelatin

½ cup boiling water

½ cup orange juice

1 (8-oz.) can crushed pineapple, drained

½ cup shredded coconut

½ cup grape halves

1 cup mini marshmallows

1 (10-oz.) can mandarin orange segments, rinsed and drained

1 (8-oz.) can whipped topping

> **Yield: 4 small salads**
>
> **Prep time:** 90 minutes
>
> **Serving size:** 1 salad

1. In a large bowl, dissolve gelatin in boiling water. Add orange juice, stir, and chill for about 30 minutes or until partially set.

2. Using a whisk, whip partially set gelatin until foamy, and stir in pineapple, coconut, grapes, marshmallows, and mandarins.

3. Fold in whipped topping thoroughly, and scoop into serving dishes. Chill for 30 minutes to 1 hour before serving.

Lettuce Lingo

Folding is as gently method of stirring used to incorporate a foam (whipped ingredient) into a recipe. It can be done with a whisk or a spatula, but turns of either should be gentle and slow. The idea is to prevent the foam from deflating.

Apple-Pecan Slaw

Sweet, crunchy apples and pecans give this cabbage salad an autumnal flair.

1/2 cup sour cream

3 TB. cider vinegar

2 TB. maple syrup

1 tsp. dried thyme

1/4 tsp. kosher salt

1 red onion, sliced thin

3 stalks celery, sliced thin on the bias

1/2 head green cabbage, shredded (about 2 cups)

2 green apples, grated, skin on

2 red apples, grated, skin on

1 cup pecan pieces, toasted and cooled

Yield: 1 large salad
Prep time: 30 minutes
Serving size: 1/4 salad

1. In a large bowl, whisk together sour cream, cider vinegar, maple syrup, thyme, and salt.

2. Add onion, celery, cabbage, green apples, red apples, and pecans. Mix thoroughly and serve.

Salad Secret

Nuts are always better when toasted. The heat releases their oils and intensifies their flavor. They're best toasted on a baking sheet in the all-around heat of a 350°F oven for about 10 minutes or until they're golden and fragrant. Toasting in a sauté pan only toasts the nut in spots, leaving them blotchy and often burnt.

Citrus Salad with Poppy Seed–Yogurt Dressing

Sweet and tangy, this salad is equally at home at breakfast, lunch, or dinner.

1 cup plain yogurt

2 TB. honey

2 TB. poppy seeds

2 ruby red grapefruit, peeled and sliced into *supremes*

1 yellow grapefruit, peeled and sliced into supremes

3 navel oranges, peeled and sliced into supremes

3 blood oranges, peeled and sliced into supremes

¼ tsp. kosher salt

¼ tsp. freshly ground black pepper

¼ cup fresh mint leaves, chopped

> **Yield: 1 large salad**
>
> **Prep time:** 60 minutes
>
> **Serving size:** ¼ salad

1. In a large bowl, whisk together yogurt, honey, and poppy seeds.

2. Add ruby red grapefruit, yellow grapefruit, navel oranges, and blood oranges, and toss to coat. Chill for 30 minutes.

3. Stir in kosher salt, pepper, and mint, and serve.

Lettuce Lingo

Supreme here refers to citrus without the rind or pith. To cut a supreme, slice off the top and bottom of the citrus fruit so it stands up straight. Slice from the top of the fruit to the bottom, removing the rind and the pith completely all the way around the fruit to expose the inner fruit. Holding the fruit in your hand over a bowl, slice to the center on both sides of every membrane that divides each section, and the supremes should fall out. (They look like naked sections.)

Grapefruit and Avocado Salad

Pink grapefruits give this salad a beautiful look, which matches its cool and creamy taste. If you can find them, use the sweet and meaty Texas ruby red grapefruits.

½ tsp. cracked pink peppercorns

½ tsp. freshly ground black pepper

Zest and juice of 2 limes

3 TB. olive oil

2 ripe avocados, sliced in wedges

2 large pink grapefruits, sectioned into supremes

½ tsp. kosher salt

> **Yield: 4 small salads**
>
> **Prep time:** 20 minutes
>
> **Serving size:** 1 salad

1. In a large bowl, whisk together peppercorns, pepper, lime zest, lime juice, and olive oil.

2. Alternately arrange avocado wedges and grapefruit supremes on a platter, drizzle with dressing, sprinkle with kosher salt, and serve.

Salad Secret

A ripe avocado should be firm but still give just a bit to the touch. Overly ripe avocados, like those used for guacamole, won't hold their shape well in this recipe. If you have a choice, pick the Hass avocado, with the thick alligator skin.

Pears with Roquefort with Pecans

Sweet pears and salty Roquefort cheese are a classic combination. Combined with a tangy dressing and sweet, crunchy nuts, this salad is an explosion of flavor.

1½ cups pecan halves

¼ cup brown sugar

1 tsp. kosher salt

¼ tsp. ground cinnamon

¼ tsp. freshly ground white pepper

¼ tsp. cayenne

2 TB. butter

1 clove garlic, minced

2 scallions, minced

1 tsp. Dijon mustard

¼ cup crumbled *Roquefort* cheese

½ tsp. freshly ground black pepper

3 TB. balsamic vinegar

1 TB. honey

⅓ cup olive oil

4 cups mixed baby greens

3 Bartlett or d'Anjou pears, sliced into thin wedges

Yield: 1 large salad
Prep time: 30 minutes
Cook time: 10 minutes
Serving size: ¼ salad

1. In a small bowl, combine pecans, brown sugar, ½ teaspoon kosher salt, cinnamon, white pepper, and cayenne.

2. In a sauté pan over medium heat, melt butter until sizzling. Add nut mixture, and stir constantly for about 3 to 5 minutes or until sugar is melted and nuts are toasted. Pour onto a baking sheet in a single layer to cool.

3. In a large bowl, combine garlic, scallions, Dijon mustard, Roquefort cheese, remaining ¹/₂ teaspoon salt, and black pepper. Mix well with a fork until creamy. Add balsamic vinegar, honey, and olive oil, and blend well.

4. In a salad bowl, combine lettuce and pears. Add enough dressing to lightly coat, and toss thoroughly. Serve topped with candied pecans.

Lettuce Lingo

Roquefort is the oldest blue cheese, favored by the ancient Romans 2,000 years ago. It comes from the Aquitaine region of southwest France, where it's made from sheep's milk and cured in limestone caves. A tale is told of a shepherd who left a hunk of bread and sheep's milk cheese in such a cave. When he found it later, although it was covered with mold, he pronounced it delicious!

Tropical Fruit Slaw

The combination of sweet fruit and salty soy sauce makes ordinary slaw exotically extraordinary.

1 TB. soy sauce

1/3 cup rice vinegar

1 tsp. freshly grated ginger

1 tsp. sesame seeds

1/3 cup canola oil

1/4 cup fresh cilantro, chopped

1/2 head napa cabbage, shredded (about 2 cups)

1/2 fresh pineapple, diced, or 1 (15-oz.) can diced pineapple, drained

1 large ripe mango, peeled and sliced into wedges

1 large ripe Hawaiian papaya, peeled, seeded, and diced

3 kiwi fruit, peeled and diced

1 cup macadamia nuts, chopped and toasted

Yield: 1 large salad
Prep time: 40 minutes
Serving size: 1/4 salad

1. In a small bowl, whisk together soy sauce, rice vinegar, ginger, sesame seeds, canola oil, and cilantro.

2. In a large salad bowl, combine cabbage, pineapple, mango, papaya, and kiwi. Add enough dressing to lightly coat, and toss well. Serve topped with macadamia nuts.

Salad Secret

Sesame seeds come in many forms, including raw and toasted. If you happen to find black sesame seeds, give them a try. They taste the same but make a more striking presentation.

Part 3

The Main Event

Salads need not be relegated to the sidelines. Today, a salad can steal the show, filling expectations and tummies.

With increased awareness of nutritional needs—and decreased time in which to prepare healthful meals—salads are an excellent choice for the home cook. In Part 3's chapters, you find salads that can be served as the main focus of a meal: salads made from hearty pasta, beans, and grains; salads loaded with meat and seafood; and even salads that cover it all, filling all your nutritional needs in every forkful. Add the fact that they're all easily and quickly prepared, and you have a recipe for a success.

Chapter 8

Meat and Seafood Salads

In This Chapter

♦ Old favorites from the salad Hall of Fame

♦ New twists on familiar flavors

♦ Exotic combinations to tempt your tummy

Meat- and fish-based salads are delicious, but they're also team players. Most of the recipes in this chapter are equally at home between two slices of bread, wrapped in a tortilla, or stuffed into pocket bread as they are on a salad plate.

One reason for the popularity of meat and fish salads is their ability to use up leftovers. Although today many a chef cooks meat specifically for use in a salad, most of these recipes were created on a shoestring. Throughout culinary history, stretching a dollar and pinching a penny has been the impetus for new recipes.

Time-Saving Salad Prep

Many people dismiss meat and fish salads when planning a menu because the thought of cooking the meat seems like a lot of work. True, cooking meat can add a substantial amount of time to the prep of a recipe. But that doesn't necessarily have to be the case. With a few time-saving measures, you can prepare meat and fish salads at the spur of the moment.

Can It!

A number of well-made canned meat products are readily available and easy to stock in your pantry for meat salads in a jiffy. Tuna, chicken, salmon, and crab are the obvious members of the can club, but you can also find canned products such as squid, octopus, turkey, beef, and ham.

What's more, many meats are available frozen and can live unopened for months in your freezer until inspiration strikes.

Plan It!

With a little forethought, you can prepare extra meat one night so you can use the leftovers for a salad the next night. For example, when you're grilling is a great time to cook a little extra and save the rest for later.

Refrigerate cooked meat for 2 or 3 days, or freeze it for a couple weeks, until you need it.

Salade Niçoise

This salad is made in the style of Nice, a city in France on the Côte d'Azure. The tuna, anchovy, olives, and herbs create a typical Mediterranean flavor.

½ lb. red new potatoes

½ lb. green beans or *haricot vert*, trimmed

1 cup extra-virgin olive oil

3 TB. red wine vinegar

1 TB. lemon juice

1 clove garlic, minced

¼ cup flat leaf parsley, chopped

¼ tsp. kosher salt

¼ tsp. freshly ground black pepper

4 cups mixed salad greens, washed and dried

1 large ripe tomato, cut into wedges

2 hard-boiled eggs, peeled and quartered

1 (6-oz.) can tuna, drained

½ cup black *niçoise olives*, pitted

12 anchovy fillets

Yield: 4 small salads
Prep time: 30 minutes
Cook time: 40 minutes
Serving size: 1 salad

1. In a large saucepan, cover potatoes with cold water and bring to a boil over high heat. Reduce heat to medium, and simmer for about 20 minutes or until tender. Drain potatoes and submerge in a bowl of ice water until cool. Cut cooled potatoes into quarters, leaving skin on.

2. In a small saucepan, cover green beans with cold water and bring to a boil over high heat. Boil for 3 minutes, drain, and immediately submerge in a bowl of ice water until cool.

3. In a small bowl, combine olive oil, red wine vinegar, lemon juice, garlic, parsley, kosher salt, and pepper. Add potatoes and green beans, toss to coat evenly, and set aside.

Lettuce Lingo

Haricot vert are small, thin, French green beans. **Niçoise olives** are similar in flavor and appearance to the black kalamata olives, but much smaller.

4. Divide salad greens evenly among 4 plates. Divide tomato, eggs, tuna, potatoes, green beans, and nicçoise olives, and arrange in sections on top of lettuce. Drizzle remaining dressing on top, and garnish each salad with 3 anchovy fillets. Serve immediately.

Deviled Ham Salad

Made with fine-quality ham, this salty, smoky salad is pleasantly satisfying. Serve it on a bed of spicy arugula, or try it on top of crackers or sliced cucumbers as a canapé.

¼ cup mayonnaise

1 TB. Dijon mustard

1 stalk celery, diced fine

3 scallions, minced

2 TB. flat leaf (Italian) parsley, minced

2 cups finely minced ham, preferably Smithfield or Black Forest

½ tsp. freshly ground black pepper

Tabasco sauce

4 cups arugula

Yield: 4 small salads
Prep time: 10 minutes
Serving size: 1 salad

1. In a large bowl, combine mayonnaise, Dijon mustard, celery, scallions, and parsley.

2. Add ham, pepper, and Tabasco sauce, and stir to combine.

3. Divide arugula among serving plates, top with deviled ham, and serve.

Tasty Morsel _____

This ham is called "deviled" because it's hot and spicy. Historically, dishes that include mustard, peppers, and other piquant spices are referred to as "deviled," "diablo," or some variant, presumably because of the fiery hot place the devil resides.

Antipasto Salad

The key to this salad is in the selection of the ingredients. In addition to using good-quality produce, be sure to pick the finest salami, the most fragrant olives, the spiciest peppers, and the best-quality Parmesan cheese.

2 cloves garlic, minced

$1/2$ tsp. fresh oregano, minced

$1/2$ tsp. fennel seed, toasted and ground

3 TB. red wine vinegar

1 large ripe tomato, diced fine

$1/4$ tsp. kosher salt

$1/4$ tsp. freshly ground black pepper

$1/4$ cup olive oil

1 large head romaine lettuce, chopped

1 cup fresh basil leaves

1 small red onion, sliced thin

1 bulb fennel root, shaved thin

$1/4$ lb. Italian salami, sliced thin and julienned

1 cup pitted kalamata olives

1 cup drained peperoncini peppers

1 cup roasted red bell peppers, homemade or jarred

1 (14-oz.) can water-packed artichoke hearts, drained

$1/2$ cup Parmesan cheese, shaved

Yield: 1 large salad
Prep time: 30 minutes
Serving size: $1/4$ salad

1. In a small bowl, combine garlic, oregano, fennel seed, red wine vinegar, tomato, kosher salt, and pepper. Add olive oil, mix well, and set aside.

2. In a salad bowl, combine lettuce, basil, red onion, fennel root, and salami. Add dressing to taste, toss well, and divide evenly among plates.

3. Evenly divide olives, peperoncini, red bell peppers, and artichoke hearts, and artfully arrange over salad. Top with shaved Parmesan and serve.

Tasty Morsel _____

Anti means "before," and traditional Italian antipasto is served before the pasta, as an appetizer. Comprised of cured meats, fresh and marinated vegetables, and cheese, these dishes were meant to be nibbled over with friends, adding an important social aspect to the meal

Avocado Shrimp Salad

Creamy avocado, crunchy veggies, and salty shrimp makes this dish Californian as they come. You can feel the sunshine with every bite.

1 TB. Dijon mustard

2 TB. white wine vinegar

¼ tsp. kosher salt

¼ tsp. freshly ground black pepper

¼ cup flat leaf parsley, chopped

3 TB. olive oil

4 cups baby mixed greens

2 ripe avocados

Juice of 2 limes

2 cups mayonnaise

2 TB. Tabasco sauce

3 TB. fresh chives, minced

2 scallions, chopped

2 stalks celery, diced fine

2 cups cooked bay shrimp

> **Yield: 4 small salads**
>
> **Prep time:** 30 minutes
>
> **Serving size:** 1 salad

1. In a small bowl, combine Dijon mustard, white wine vinegar, kosher salt, pepper, parsley, and olive oil. Add mixed greens, toss, and divide evenly among serving plates.

2. Slice avocadoes in half lengthwise, and remove pits. Lay cut side down and slice off a small bit on the top rounded edge (this prevents avocado from rocking when set cut side up). Squeeze juice of 1 lime over exposed fruit to prevent browning. Set 1 avocado ½ in the center of each plate, on top of mixed green salad.

3. In a large bowl, combine mayonnaise, remaining lime juice, Tabasco sauce, 2 tablespoons chives, scallions, and celery. Mix well, and fold in shrimp. Divide evenly among avocados, filling in each pit hole and mounding gently. Serve immediately, topped with remaining 1 tablespoon chives.

Variation: If you can't find good avocados anywhere, you can replace them with large, hollowed-out tomatoes in this recipe.

Salad Secret _____

Markets often stock unripened avocados, so buy them 2 or 3 days ahead to be sure you get a ripe one. Then leave them at room temperature until you need them.

Grilled Shrimp Salad

This flavorful dish benefits from a long marinade to accentuate the sweet and spicy flavors. Plan ahead for optimal results.

1 bunch cilantro (about 3 cups, including stems)

Zest and juice of 4 medium limes

3 cloves garlic, minced

$\frac{1}{2}$ cup orange marmalade

1 TB. Green Tabasco sauce

$\frac{1}{4}$ cup soy sauce

1 cup orange juice

$\frac{1}{2}$ cup olive oil

1 lb. large shrimp, shelled and deveined

2 large tomatoes, diced

2 red bell peppers, roasted, peeled, seeded, and diced

1 small jicama, peeled and diced

1 large cucumber, diced

1 avocado, diced

4 cups arugula

Yield: 1 large salad
Prep time: 30 minutes, plus 1 to 3 hours to marinate
Cook time: 10 minutes
Serving size: ¼ salad

1. Remove 1 cup leaves from cilantro and reserve. Mince remaining bunch, including stems, and place in a large bowl. Whisk in lime zest, lime juice, garlic, orange marmalade, Green Tabasco sauce, soy sauce, orange juice, and olive oil. Pour off 1 cup, and set aside.

2. Add shrimp to remaining dressing, toss well, and marinate for 1 to 3 hours or overnight.

3. Preheat the broiler, or a grill, on high heat. Soak 6 to 8 wooden skewers in water for at least 30 minutes.

4. Thread shrimp onto skewers and grill for 2 or 3 minutes per side or until golden brown. Set aside.

5. In a salad bowl, combine reserved dressing, reserved cilantro leaves, tomatoes, roasted bell peppers, jicama, cucumber, avocado, and arugula. Toss well and divide among serving plates.

6. Remove shrimp from the skewers, place on top of salads, and serve.

Salad Secret

You can buy roasted bell peppers ready-made in jars. Look for them in the pickle aisle. You can also make your own by placing them directly onto the flame of a gas burner or under a broiler. Rotate until completely blackened, place in a plastic bag, and seal to create steam. When cool, rub off the skin, remove the seeds, and slice.

Crab Louie Salad

This crisp, crunchy salad has a hint of the sea in every forkful.

1 cup mayonnaise

2 TB. chili sauce

1 hard-boiled egg, chopped fine

½ green bell pepper, ribs and seeds removed, and chopped fine

1 (4-oz.) can chopped pimento

2 TB. flat leaf parsley, chopped

2 scallions, chopped

2 cups cooked crabmeat

2 cups shredded iceberg lettuce

1 large tomato, sliced in wedges

2 TB. chopped fresh chives

Yield: 4 small salads
Prep time: 20 minutes
Serving size: 1 salad

1. In a large bowl, stir together mayonnaise, chili sauce, hard-boiled egg, green bell pepper, pimento, parsley, and scallions. Add crabmeat and toss.

2. Divide lettuce evenly among serving plates. Top with crab salad and tomato wedges. Sprinkle with chopped chives and serve.

Tasty Morsel

This salad is thought to have originated in San Francisco in the early 1900s. Today, you can still buy fresh cracked crab along the docks at Fisherman's Wharf. Make it at home with fresh or canned crab. Forget the fake stuff; it doesn't do the salad justice.

Caesar Salad *(Chapter 3)*.

Baby Greens Salad *(Chapter 3)*.

Artichoke Heart Salad *(Chapter 4)*.

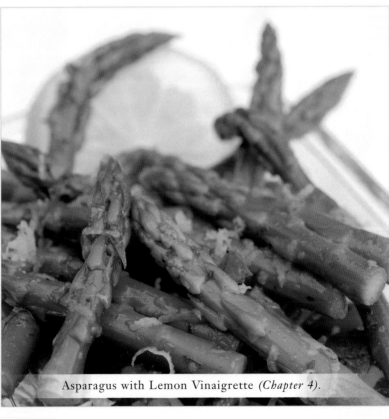

Asparagus with Lemon Vinaigrette *(Chapter 4)*.

Caprese Salad *(Chapter 4).*

Warm Beet and Berry Salad *(Chapter 5).*

Warm Brussels Sprout Salad *(Chapter 5)*.

Warm Pumpkin and Bacon Salad *(Chapter 5)*.

Winter Bean Salad *(Chapter 5)*.

Curry Potato Salad *(Chapter 6)*.

Dilly Potato Salad *(Chapter 6)*.

Red Potato Salad with Stilton *(Chapter 6)*.

Sweet Potato and Pecan Salad *(Chapter 6)*.

Waldorf Salad *(Chapter 7)*.

Grapefruit and Avocado Salad *(Chapter 7).*

Tropical Fruit Slaw *(Chapter 7).*

Salad Niçoise *(Chapter 8)*.

Antipasto Salad *(Chapter 8)*.

Grilled Shrimp Salad *(Chapter 8)*.

Thai Chicken Salad *(Chapter 8)*.

Pesto Pasta Salad *(Chapter 9)*.

Seafood Pasta Salad *(Chapter 9)*.

Japanese Soba Salad *(Chapter 9)*.

Orzo Salad *(Chapter 9)*.

Brown Rice and Golden Raisin Salad
(Chapter 10).

Confetti Couscous *(Chapter 10)*.

Quinoa-Herb Salad *(Chapter 10)*.

Asian Bean Sprout Salad *(Chapter 11)*.

Cuban Grilled Corn and Black Bean Salad
(Chapter 11).

Tofu-Veggie Salad *(Chapter 11)*.

White Bean Salad *(Chapter 11)*.

Southwestern Steak Salad
(Chapter 12).

Italian Bread Salad *(Chapter 12).*

Middle Eastern Cucumber, Pita,
and Bean Salad *(Chapter 12).*

Creamy Salmon and Dill Salad

For a fish, salmon has a fairly sweet and creamy texture. Combined with the creamy, dilly dressing in this salad, and it's heaven on a fork.

1 TB. Dijon mustard

½ cup sour cream

¼ cup mayonnaise

2 large lemons

1 bunch fresh dill, minced (about 1 cup)

1 tsp. dried dill

½ tsp. kosher salt

½ tsp. freshly ground black pepper

1 (15-oz.) can salmon, or 1 lb. home-cooked salmon, flaked

1 large cucumber, peeled, seeded, and diced

3 scallions, chopped

3 stalks celery, chopped

2 large roma tomatoes, diced

5 or 6 radishes, sliced

1 TB. olive oil

1 TB. white wine vinegar

4 cups mixed baby greens

> **Yield: 4 small salads**
> **Prep time:** 30 minutes
> **Serving size:** 1 salad

1. In a large bowl, stir together Dijon mustard, sour cream, mayonnaise, zest and juice of 1 lemon, fresh dill, dried dill, kosher salt, and pepper.

2. Add salmon, cucumber, scallions, celery, tomatoes, and radishes, and toss well to combine.

3. In a separate bowl, combine olive oil, white wine vinegar, and baby greens. Toss together and divide evenly among serving plates. Top with a generous helping of salmon salad. Cut remaining lemon into wedges to garnish, and serve.

Tasty Morsel

Dill has been used since the Middle Ages as an herbal remedy to relieve upset stomachs and gas ... and to protect against witchcraft

Mixed Seafood Salad

This salad's classic seaside flavor comes not just from the fish, but from the addition of Old Bay seasoning. A spice blend from the Chesapeake Bay, Old Bay is the perfect sweet and spicy blend of celery seeds, bay, mustard, cinnamon, and ginger.

¼ lb. bay scallops

¼ lb. bay shrimp

¼ lb. cod or other firm, mild, whitefish, diced

¼ lb. calamari, diced

¼ lb. salmon, diced

3 cloves garlic, minced

1 TB. Dijon mustard

1 TB. tomato paste

1 tsp. Old Bay seasoning

2 lemons

3 TB. rice vinegar

¼ cup olive oil

¼ tsp. kosher salt

¼ tsp. freshly ground black pepper

½ head napa cabbage, chopped (about 2 cups)

½ small red onion, diced

3 medium roma tomatoes, diced

Yield: 1 large salad
Prep time: 30 minutes
Cook time: 15 minutes
Serving size: ¼ salad

1. Fill a large bowl ½ full with ice water.

2. Bring a large pot of water to a rolling boil over high heat. In batches, add scallops, shrimp, cod, calamari, and salmon, and cook 2 or 3 minutes until opaque. Quickly drain and plunge into ice water to stop cooking. When cool, drain and set aside.

3. In a large bowl, whisk together garlic, Dijon mustard, tomato paste, Old Bay seasoning, zest and juice of 1 lemon, rice vinegar, olive oil, kosher salt, and pepper.

4. Add seafood, cabbage, red onion, and tomatoes, and toss well. Slice remaining lemon into wedges for garnish, and serve.

Heads-Up!

It's easy to overcook the seafood in this recipe, so watch it carefully and stop the cooking as soon as the colors change. If it cooks too long, your seafood will be tough and rubbery.

Lobster Salad

Sweet lobster meat and the delicate, licorice essence of fennel make the perfect pair in this salad.

½ cup mayonnaise

1 tsp. prepared horseradish

2 lemons

¼ cup fresh tarragon, minced

¼ tsp. kosher salt

1 (4-oz.) jar diced pimentos

1 lb. lobster meat, cooked and diced

2 scallions, minced

1 bulb fennel, shaved thin

3 cucumbers, shaved thin

1 TB. olive oil

1 TB. tarragon vinegar

Yield: 4 small salads

Prep time: 30 minutes, plus 30 minutes to chill

Serving size: 1 salad

1. In a large bowl, stir together mayonnaise, horseradish, zest and juice of 1 lemon, tarragon, kosher salt, and pimentos.

2. Add lobster meat and scallions, and toss. Chill 30 minutes.

3. In a separate bowl, toss fennel and cucumbers with olive oil and tarragon vinegar. Divide evenly among serving plates, and top with a generous serving of lobster salad.

4. Slice remaining lemon into wedges for garnish, and serve.

Tasty Morsel

Sweet lobster meat is thought of as a luxury item today, but when the first settlers arrived in New England, lobsters were so prevalent that they were considered a poor man's food, and they were used to bait other fish. To cook one, plop it (live) in boiling water. This will cool the water. When the water returns to the boil, cover and cook 12 minutes. Drain, cool, and remove the meat.

Orange Chicken Salad

Juicy, sweet, and acidic, citrus fruits are the perfect accompaniment to chicken.

Zest and juice of 1 lime (about 1 TB. juice)

Zest and juice of 1 lemon (about 2 TB. juice)

¼ cup fresh mint, chopped

1 cup green onions, chopped

1 TB. poppy seeds

1 TB. honey

½ tsp. kosher salt

½ tsp. freshly ground black pepper

½ cup olive oil

3 cups cooked chicken breast, shredded

2 sweet oranges, peeled, sectioned, and diced

3 mandarins or tangerines, peeled, sectioned, and diced

1 ruby red grapefruit, peeled, sectioned, and diced

2 blood oranges, peeled, sectioned, and diced

Yield: 1 large salad
Prep time: 30 minutes, plus 1 hour cooling time
Serving size: ¼ salad

1. In a large bowl, whisk together lime zest, lime juice, lemon zest, lemon juice, mint, green onions, poppy seeds, honey, kosher salt, pepper, and olive oil.

2. Add chicken, oranges, mandarins, grapefruit, and blood oranges, and toss to coat. Cover and refrigerate at least 1 hour to allow flavors to mingle.

3. Serve chilled.

Tasty Morsel

If the unusual citrus fruits are nowhere to be found, this salad tastes great with simple oranges, too. You can pump up the color with the addition of some raspberries or pomegranate seeds.

Thai Chicken Salad

Thai food is known for its simultaneous use of spicy, sour, sweet, and salty flavors. You'll find them all in this exotic salad.

2 TB. peanut oil

1 TB. chile oil

2 cloves garlic, minced

1 TB. fresh ginger, grated

Zest and juice of 2 large limes

¼ cup coconut milk

¼ cup Thai or Vietnamese *fish sauce*, or soy sauce

4 cups cooked chicken, diced or shredded

2 medium carrots, grated

2 scallions, sliced thin on an angle

2 cucumbers, grated

1 small red onion, sliced thin

¼ cup fresh cilantro leaves

¼ cup peanuts, chopped

Yield: 4 small salads

Prep time: 60 minutes, plus 30 to 60 minutes cooling time

Serving size: 1 salad

1. In a large bowl, whisk together peanut oil, chile oil, garlic, ginger, lime zest, lime juice, coconut milk, and fish sauce.

2. Add chicken, carrots, scallions, cucumbers, red onion, and cilantro. Toss thoroughly to coat.

3. Divide among plates, top with peanuts, and serve.

Lettuce Lingo

Fish sauce is a liquid condiment, similar in appearance to soy sauce, made from fermented raw or dried fish. Although it may smell fishy, the fish flavor cooks away, adding a rich, deep, complex flavor to recipes.

Chapter 9

Pasta Salads

In This Chapter

- ◆ Fun with pasta shapes
- ◆ Cooking up international flavors
- ◆ Old favorites and new classics

The origin of pasta is the subject of some debate, but the first pasta or noodles were likely nothing more than dried gruel. Grains mixed to a paste, rolled thin and dried, were the first attempts at grain preservation. Such foods were found to be portable and nutritious, perfect for travelers.

Every culture has its own form of pasta, made from many types of grains and starches, including rice, potato, buckwheat, millet, and soy. Italian pasta (meaning "paste") is made from high-protein Durham wheat and is the most widely available. While Durham has high protein, the processing of it diminishes much of the nutritional value. Whole-wheat pasta is fairly common now and is available in a wide assortment of shapes and sizes.

Cooking Pasta

The secret to cooking pasta properly is to use plenty of water. Choose a large pot that holds at least 5 quarts, and be sure the water is at a full rolling boil before adding the pasta. When the pasta goes in, the water will stop boiling momentarily. Immediately stir it around to keep the pasta from sinking and sticking.

Salad Secret

Some cooks add oil to pasta water. That oil will only rise to the top and do nothing to prevent pasta from sticking. Tossing the finished pasta with a little oil after draining, however, does help keep it loose.

It's easy to overcook pasta. These following recipes refer to the term *al dente*, which literally means "to the tooth," not "chewy" as many believe. Pasta, and often vegetables, are described this way when they're cooked through but still maintain a little texture. The purpose of the term is to remind cooks that pasta and vegetables should not be cooked until mushy.

Although the pasta may be cooked the proper length of time, it can become overcooked if it sits around waiting to be added to a recipe. To prevent overcooking, rinse the al dente pasta with cold water as soon as it's drained. This ensures it maintains the perfect texture.

Different Pasta Shapes

Dozens of pasta shapes are available, and although most recipes indicate a specific shape, you can often get creative and choose something different.

In general, thin noodles go with thin sauces and dressings. The delicate texture of angel hair or orzo, for example, can easily be overpowered by thick, heavy sauces. Chunkier toppings benefit from thick noodles or pasta with ridges and crevices that can hold onto all the goodies.

Italian Pasta Salad

You can use any shape pasta for this recipe, but rotini is the best at holding on to the crisp, fresh vegetables and garlicky herb dressing.

½ cup olive oil

2 TB. red wine vinegar

2 cloves garlic, minced

1 TB. Italian seasoning

Pinch kosher salt

1 lb. uncooked *rotini* pasta

1 medium red onion, chopped

2 ripe tomatoes, diced

1 red bell pepper, ribs and seeds removed, and diced

½ cup grated Parmesan cheese

1 cup fresh basil leaves, minced

Yield: 1 large salad

Prep time: 40 minutes

Cook time: 20 minutes

Serving size: ¼ salad

1. In a large salad bowl, whisk together olive oil, red wine vinegar, garlic, and Italian seasoning.

2. In a large saucepan over high heat, bring 4 quarts water to a full rolling boil. Add pinch salt and rotini. Stir briefly, and cook for about 12 minutes or until al dente. Drain, rinse with cold water, and add to dressing.

3. Add onion, tomatoes, and red bell pepper, and toss thoroughly. Cover and chill at least 30 minutes.

4. Stir in Parmesan cheese and basil just before serving.

Salad Secret _____

Making your own spice mixes is easy and cheaper than the store-bought versions. To make Italian seasoning for this recipe, stir together ¼ cup fresh chopped oregano, ¼ cup fresh chopped basil, ¼ cup ground fennel seed, 2 tablespoons fresh chopped sage, 2 tablespoons fresh chopped rosemary, and 3 minced cloves garlic. Store in the refrigerator for up to a week or in the freezer for 1 month.

Pesto Pasta Salad

Spicy, salty, and full of basil, this classic concoction is just as good cold as it is hot.

Pinch plus ½ tsp. kosher salt

1 lb. uncooked *orecchietti*

1 cup Pesto Sauce (recipe later in this chapter)

¼ cup sliced kalamata olives

1 cup fresh or frozen peas, defrosted if frozen

2 cups cherry tomatoes, halved

½ tsp. freshly ground black pepper

¼ cup pine nuts or walnuts

1 cup fresh basil leaves, chopped

¼ cup shaved Parmesan cheese

Yield: 1 large salad
Prep time: 40 minutes
Cook time: 20 minutes
Serving size: ¼ salad

1. In a large saucepan over high heat, bring 4 quarts water to a full rolling boil. Add pinch salt and orecchietti. Stir briefly, and cook for about 12 minutes or until al dente. Drain, rinse with cold water, and pour into a large salad bowl.

Lettuce Lingo

In Italian, *orecchio* means "ear," and **orecchietti** pasta is meant to resemble little ears.

2. Add Pesto Sauce to pasta, and stir to thoroughly combine. Toss in olives, peas, tomatoes, remaining ½ teaspoon kosher salt, and pepper, and chill for at least 30 minutes.

3. Serve chilled, topped with pine nuts, basil, and Parmesan cheese.

Pesto Sauce

This garlicky, herby sauce is great to make in large batches so you have some on hand to use at a moment's notice.

3 cloves garlic, minced

3 cups fresh basil leaves

½ cup pine nuts or walnuts

½ cup olive oil

¼ cup Parmesan cheese

¼ tsp. kosher salt

> **Yield: about 1½ cups**
> **Prep time:** 15 minutes
> **Serving size:** ¼ cup

1. In a food processor fitted with a steel blade, combine garlic, basil, and pine nuts until a smooth paste forms.

2. With the machine on, slowly drizzle in olive oil, and add Parmesan cheese and kosher salt.

3. Use immediately, refrigerate for up to a week, or freeze for several months.

Tasty Morsel

Pesto is an ancient sauce, traditionally made in a mortar and pestle, which is where it gets its name *pesto*.

Seafood Pasta Salad

Pasta shells are the perfect base to hold this salad's seaside flavors. The salty capers and anchovies accent the sweet, juicy seafood.

3 anchovy fillets, mashed

2 cloves garlic, minced

1 TB. capers

3 scallions, chopped

Juice of 1 lemon

¼ tsp. red chile flakes

¼ tsp. plus pinch kosher salt

2 TB. tarragon vinegar

3 TB. olive oil

1 lb. uncooked shell pasta

½ lb. bay shrimp, cooked

½ lb. cooked crabmeat or 1 (6-oz.) can crabmeat

½ lb. salmon meat, cooked and flaked, or 1 (7.5-oz.) can salmon meat

½ small red onion, chopped

2 heads Belgian endive, chopped (about 2 cups)

1 lemon, cut into wedges

Yield: 1 large salad
Prep time: 40 minutes
Cook time: 20 minutes
Serving size: ¼ salad

1. In a large bowl, whisk together anchovies, garlic, capers, scallions, zest and juice of 1 lemon, red chile flakes, ¼ teaspoon kosher salt, tarragon vinegar, and olive oil.

2. In a large saucepan over high heat, bring 4 quarts water to a full rolling boil. Add pinch salt and shell pasta. Stir briefly, and cook for about 12 minutes or until al dente. Drain, rinse with cold water, and add to dressing.

3. Add shrimp, crabmeat, salmon, onion, and Belgian endive, and toss thoroughly. Chill for at least 30 minutes before serving with lemon wedges.

Salad Secret _____

This dish calls out for sourdough. Serve it in a hollowed-out sourdough loaf, with sourdough croutons, or make it into a sourdough sandwich. Delish fish!

Chinese Noodle Salad

This sweet, gingery dressing is a step above the usual super-salty ramen sauce.

2 cloves garlic, minced

2 TB. soy sauce

2 TB. rice vinegar

1 TB. honey

1 TB. fresh ginger, grated

1 TB. sesame oil

1 TB. peanut oil

Zest and juice of 1 orange

1 TB. sesame seeds

Pinch kosher salt

2 (3-oz.) pkg. ramen noodles

1 cup bean sprouts

3 scallions, chopped

1 carrot, grated

5 or 6 radishes, sliced

½ cup fresh cilantro leaves

½ cup peanuts or cashews, chopped

Yield: 1 large salad
Prep time: 40 minutes
Cook time: 10 minutes
Serving size: ¼ salad

1. In a large bowl, whisk together garlic, soy sauce, rice vinegar, honey, ginger, sesame oil, peanut oil, orange zest, orange juice, and sesame seeds.

2. In a large saucepan over high heat, bring 2 quarts water to a full rolling boil. Add pinch salt and ramen noodles. (Discard flavor packet.) Stir briefly, and cook for about 3 minutes. Drain, rinse with cold water, and add to dressing.

Salad Secret

Add cooked chicken or shrimp to this salad for a fantastic luncheon dish.

3. Add bean sprouts, scallions, carrot, and radishes. Toss to coat thoroughly, and chill for at least 30 minutes.

4. Top with cilantro and peanuts just before serving.

Japanese Soba Salad

Spicy wasabi, earthy mushrooms, and crunchy diakon radish give this salad a definitive Japanese flair.

1 TB. wasabi paste

1 TB. black sesame seeds

2 TB. tamari

3 TB rice vinegar

½ tsp. sugar

3 TB. peanut oil

2 stalks celery

1 cup diakon, grated

1 cup enoki mushrooms

1 cup shiitake mushrooms

Pinch kosher salt

1 lb. uncooked soba noodles

3 scallions, chopped

Yield: 1 large salad
Prep time: 40 minutes
Cook time: 20 minutes
Serving size: ¼ salad

1. In a large bowl, whisk together wasabi paste, sesame seeds, tamari, rice vinegar, sugar, and peanut oil.

2. Add celery, daikon, enoki mushrooms, and shiitake mushrooms.

3. In a large saucepan over high heat, bring 2 quarts water to a full rolling boil. Add pinch salt and soba noodles. Stir briefly, and bring back to the boil for 2 or 3 minutes. Add 1 cup cold water if necessary to prevent boiling over. Drain and rinse well with cold water.

4. Add cool, rinsed noodles to dressing. Toss thoroughly, and chill at least 30 minutes before serving, topped with chopped scallions.

Salad Secret

Soba is a thin Japanese noodle made from buckwheat. It's used both hot in brothy soups and cold in salads. If you're feeling adventurous, you can make this recipe with udon, another Japanese noodle. Udon noodles are thicker and are usually made from wheat.

Mediterranean Pasta Salad

The flavors of the Mediterranean—herbs, vegetables, salty olives, fish, and cheese—blossom in this fresh and hearty salad.

3 anchovy fillets, smashed

2 cloves garlic, minced

1 TB. capers

1 tsp. herbes de Provence

Zest and juice of 1 lemon

3 TB. olive oil

3 large roma tomatoes, diced

1 large zucchini, grated

1 (15-oz.) can artichoke hearts (not marinated)

Pinch kosher salt

1 lb. uncooked penne pasta

2 cups haricot verts or green string beans

¼ cup *niçoise olives*, pitted

¼ lb. goat cheese, crumbled

Yield: 1 large salad
Prep time: 40 minutes
Cook time: 20 minutes
Serving size: ¼ salad

1. In a large bowl, combine anchovies, garlic, capers, herbes de Provence, lemon zest, lemon juice, and olive oil.

2. Add tomatoes, zucchini, and artichoke hearts, and toss to coat.

Lettuce Lingo

Nicçoise olives come from the Provence region of France and are a key ingredient in Salade Niçoise. They're characterized by their tiny size, purple/black color, and slightly sour tang. Kalamata olives can be substituted quite successfully.

3. In a large saucepan over high heat, bring 4 quarts water to a full rolling boil. Add pinch salt and penne. Stir briefly, and cook for about 10 minutes or until nearly al dente. Add haricot verts, and cook for 2 more minutes. Drain, rinse with cold water, and add to dressing. Mix thoroughly.

4. Chill at least 30 minutes. Before serving, mix in olives and goat cheese.

Orzo Salad

The pasta is Italian, but the recipe is reminiscent of Greece, with fresh mint, crunchy veggies, and feta cheese.

2 cloves garlic

¼ cup fresh mint, minced

¼ cup fresh oregano, minced

2 TB. red wine vinegar

3 TB. olive oil

¼ tsp. plus pinch kosher salt

¼ tsp. freshly ground black pepper

½ cup kalamata olives, chopped

1 small red onion, chopped

1 large cucumber, diced

2 large roma tomatoes, diced

1 lb. uncooked *orzo* pasta

¼ lb. feta cheese

Yield: 1 large salad
Prep time: 20 minutes
Cook time: 20 minutes
Serving size: ¼ salad

1. In a large bowl, combine garlic, mint, oregano, red wine vinegar, olive oil, ¼ teaspoon kosher salt, and pepper.

2. Toss in olives, onion, cucumber, and tomatoes.

3. In a large saucepan over high heat, bring 2 quarts water to a full rolling boil. Add pinch kosher salt and orzo. Cook for 5 to 7 minutes, stirring frequently, until al dente. Drain, rinse with cold water, and add to dressing. Mix thoroughly.

4. Chill at least 30 minutes. Before serving, mix in feta cheese.

Lettuce Lingo

Orzo means "barley" in Italian, but it's really pasta. It looks a lot like thick rice, just slightly smaller than a pine nut.

Spinach Fettuccini Salad

Salty bacon adds the perfect balance to fresh, crisp spinach and sweet, tangy balsamic vinegar.

5 slices bacon, cooked and crumbled

2 cloves garlic, minced

2 TB. balsamic vinegar

3 TB. olive oil

½ lb. sliced mushrooms

1 small red onion, sliced

Pinch kosher salt

1 lb. uncooked spinach fettuccini

3 cups baby spinach leaves

3 hard-boiled eggs, peeled and sliced

Yield: 1 large salad
Prep time: 40 minutes
Cook time: 20 minutes
Serving size: ¼ salad

1. In a large bowl, combine bacon, garlic, balsamic vinegar, and olive oil.

2. Add mushrooms and onion, and mix thoroughly.

3. In a large saucepan over high heat, bring 2 quarts water and pinch salt to a full rolling boil. Break fettuccini into 2- or 3-inch pieces and add to water. Stir briefly, and cook for about 12 minutes or until al dente. Drain, rinse with cold water, and add to dressing. Mix thoroughly.

4. Chill at least 30 minutes. Before serving, mix in spinach and eggs.

Salad Secret _____

Cook your hard-boiled eggs well in advance for the best slices. They may peel more easily when they're freshly boiled, but slices don't hold their shape well until fully chilled. For best results, cook them the night before.

Chapter 10

Grain Salads

In This Chapter

- ◆ Fantastic flavors from across the globe
- ◆ Classic and modern flavor combinations
- ◆ Hearty grains blends and standout solo acts

Grain is one of the most underutilized foods we have, yet it's one of the most important foods our body needs. We eat a lot of wheat in the United States, but it's made into highly refined flour and mixed with refined sugars and hydrogenated oils until it's no longer recognizable as grain.

The processed grains found in white breads, white rice, and white flour are major contributors to poor health. Increased intake of whole-grain products can improve overall health by lowering risk of heart disease, gastrointestinal disorders, and certain forms of cancer.

The average adult should consume 8 to 11 servings of whole-grain foods a day. The portion sizes vary, but you should aim for 4 or 5 cups whole grains every day. Most American get nowhere near that amount of whole grains. Adding a couple grain-based salads to your weekly menu is a delicious way to get your grains.

Cooking Grains

The basic method of cooking grain is to boil it in water. The ratio of water to grain varies, but it's generally $2^1/_2$ to 3 parts water to 1 part grain. First the water is boiled and then the grains are added and simmered with the lid on to trap the steam, which tenderizes the grain by encouraging absorption of water. It's also possible to cook grain as you would pasta, in a huge pot of boiling water, straining out the grain when tender. This method loses some nutrients, but it's convenient if you don't know the optimal water-to-grain ratio.

Simply boiling grains works to cook them, but their flavor is greatly enhanced by toasting. Sautéed in a small amount of oil until brown and fragrant, grain takes on a nutty, rich flavor.

Tabouli

This fresh, light salad, full of parsley and lemon, is a standard item on Middle Eastern menus.

1 small white onion

1 cup *bulgur* wheat

2 cups water

Juice of 1 lemon

½ tsp. kosher salt

½ tsp. freshly ground black pepper

¼ cup olive oil

1 cup fresh Italian parsley

1 large tomato, diced

6 lemon wedges

8 to 10 spears romaine lettuce

Yield: 1 large salad

Prep time: 40 minutes

Serving size: ¼ salad

1. Chop onion and soak in cold water for 15 to 30 minutes. Drain and set aside.

2. In a large bowl, combine bulgur and water, and soak for 30 minutes or until tender. Drain thoroughly.

3. In a large bowl, whisk together lemon juice, kosher salt, pepper, and olive oil. Add parsley, onion, tomato, and bulgur, and toss to coat.

4. Serve with lemon wedges and romaine lettuce spears.

Lettuce Lingo

Bulgur is wheat that has been de-hulled and parboiled. It requires no cooking but must be soaked in water to soften. Cracked wheat, on the other hand, has not been parboiled, and therefore, must be cooked. To use it in this recipe, boil 2 cups water, reduce heat to low, add cracked wheat, cover, and simmer for 15 minutes or until tender.

Brown Rice and Golden Raisin Salad

This salad has a satisfyingly hearty flavor and texture, made all the more special by the addition of sweet and chewy golden raisins and exotic spices.

5 cups water

2 cups brown rice

2 TB. white wine vinegar

3 cloves garlic, minced

1 tsp. ground cinnamon

1 tsp. ground cumin

$\frac{1}{2}$ tsp. kosher salt

2 TB. olive oil

1 cup green onion, chopped

1 cup celery, diced

1 large carrot, grated

$\frac{1}{2}$ cup sliced almonds

$\frac{1}{2}$ cup golden raisins

Yield: 1 large salad
Prep time: 20 minutes
Cook time: 45 minutes
Serving size: $\frac{1}{4}$ salad

1. In a medium saucepan over high heat, bring water to a boil. Add rice, reduce heat to low, cover, and simmer for 45 minutes or until water is absorbed. Cool completely.

2. In a large bowl, whisk together white wine vinegar, garlic, cinnamon, cumin, kosher salt, and olive oil.

3. Add onion, celery, carrot, almonds, raisins, and cooled rice. Toss to coat and serve.

Tasty Morsel

Brown rice is nuttier, chewier, and more healthful than regular white rice. Because the bran is left on during processing, brown rice maintains vitamins and minerals no longer present in white rice, including B_1, B_3, magnesium, and iron. The bran also contains fiber and oil that can help reduce cholesterol.

Wild Rice–Zucchini Salad

The chewy texture and nutty flavor of this wild rice salad nicely comple-ments the tender, flakey meat of grilled or broiled fish.

2 TB. olive oil

2 leeks, chopped thin

1 cup wild rice

Zest of 1 lemon

½ cup sliced almonds

3 cups water

½ tsp. kosher salt

Yield: 1 large salad
Prep time: 10 minutes
Cook time: 90 minutes
Serving size: ¼ salad

1. In a large sauté pan over high heat, heat olive oil. Add leeks, and cook until tender.

2. Add wild rice, lemon zest, and almonds, and cook, stirring, for 5 to 10 minutes or until toasted and brown.

3. Add water and bring to a boil. Reduce heat to low, cover, and cook for 45 to 60 minutes or until liquid is absorbed. Remove from heat, and spread onto a baking sheet to cool.

4. Add kosher salt and fluff with a fork just before serving.

Tasty Morsel

Wild rice comes from a wild marsh grass native to the northern part of the United States. It's chewier and nuttier than regular rice and, consequently, it's commonly thought to be undercooked.

Confetti Couscous

Couscous is the perfect base for the mild, currylike spices of this salad.

2 cups instant couscous

1 cup plain yogurt

1 clove garlic, minced

1 small yellow onion, grated

2 TB. olive oil

Zest and juice of 1 lemon

1 tsp. ground cumin

1 tsp. ground coriander

1 tsp. turmeric

¼ tsp. kosher salt

¼ tsp. freshly ground white pepper

1 yellow bell pepper, ribs and seeds removed, and diced

1 large roma tomato, diced

1 large cucumber, diced

1 large carrot, grated

½ cup dried currants

½ cup sliced almonds

2 hearts of romaine lettuce, chopped

Yield: 1 large salad
Prep time: 20 minutes
Cook time: 60 minutes
Serving size: ¼ salad

1. Cook couscous according to package instructions. Fluff, and set aside to cool.

2. In a large bowl, whisk together yogurt, garlic, onion, olive oil, lemon zest, lemon juice, cumin, coriander, turmeric, kosher salt, and pepper.

3. Add yellow bell pepper, tomato, cucumber, and carrot. Chill for 30 to 60 minutes to allow flavors to mingle.

4. Add currants, almonds, and couscous, and toss thoroughly. Serve on bed of chopped romaine.

Tasty Morsel

Couscous is not actually a grain, but tiny, granular pasta made from Durham-based semolina flour. Traditional couscous must be steamed several times, but in the United States, it's mainly available in instant form and needs only boiling water and 5 to 10 minutes to cook. The finished product should always be light and fluffy and never gummy.

Green Rice Salad

This salad is fresh and herby, with a little crunch. Plus, it looks beautiful.

1 cup *watercress*, chopped

1 cup fresh cilantro, chopped

1 cup spinach, chopped

2 cups water

3 TB. olive oil

1 cup long-grain rice

2 cloves garlic

2 TB. white wine vinegar

3 scallions, chopped

2 cups green beans, trimmed and cut into ¼-in. pieces

2 cups fresh or frozen green peas (thawed if frozen)

1 cup pecan pieces, toasted and chopped

¼ cup fresh chives, chopped

¼ tsp. kosher salt

¼ tsp. freshly ground black pepper

Yield: 1 large salad
Prep time: 40 minutes
Cook time: 30 minutes
Serving size: ¼ salad

1. In a blender, combine watercress, cilantro, spinach, and 1 cup water. Cover and purée until smooth, adding more water if necessary.

2. In a large saucepan over high heat, heat 1 tablespoon olive oil. Add rice and garlic, and cook for 3 to 5 minutes or until toasted and golden brown.

3. Add purée and remaining 1 cup water, and bring to a boil. Reduce heat to low, cover, and simmer for 20 minutes or until liquid is fully absorbed. Pour out onto a baking sheet and cool completely.

4. In a large bowl, combine remaining 2 tablespoons olive oil, white wine vinegar, scallions, green beans, peas, and cooled rice. Chill at least 30 minutes.

5. Before serving, toss in pecans, chives, kosher salt, and pepper.

Lettuce Lingo

Watercress is one of the oldest-known leaf vegetables consumed by humans. The ancient Greeks believed it made them smarter, the Romans used it to cure baldness, and the Egyptians fed watercress juice to slaves to increase productivity. It has thick, hollow stems; dark green leaves; and a clean, peppery flavor.

Kasha Vinaigrette

The combination of kasha, squash, nuts, and dried fruit is not only a healthful mix, but a flavorful side dish option as well.

1⅓ cups water

½ cup *kasha*

1 large butternut squash, peeled and diced

¼ cup olive oil

1 shallot, minced

¼ tsp. ground nutmeg

1 TB. honey

½ cup fresh mint, chopped

1 TB. white wine vinegar

Zest and juice of 1 orange

1 small red onion, diced

½ cup toasted walnuts, chopped

½ cup dried cranberries

Yield: 1 large salad
Prep time: 45 minutes
Cook time: 50 minutes
Serving size: ¼ salad

1. In a large saucepan over high heat, bring water to a boil. Add kasha, reduce heat to low, cover, and simmer for 15 minutes or until tender. Drain, spread onto baking sheet, and set aside to cool completely.

2. Preheat the oven to 450°F.

3. Toss squash with 2 tablespoons olive oil, spread onto a baking sheet, and roast for about 30 minutes or until tender and golden brown. Cool completely.

4. In a large bowl, combine remaining olive oil with shallot, nutmeg, honey, mint, white wine vinegar, orange zest, and orange juice. Add cooled kasha, cooled squash, and onion. Toss well, and chill for 30 to 60 minutes.

5. Before serving, toss in walnuts and cranberries.

Lettuce Lingo

Kasha is the name given to buckwheat that's been toasted. Buckwheat is eaten as a grain, but it's actually the seed of an herb native to Russia.

Mixed-Grain Provençal

This dish is heavy with the nutty flavor and rich texture of grain. Dressed in anchovies, shallots, and mustard, it's a perfect match to full-flavored meats.

¼ cup olive oil

1 small yellow onion, chopped

1 carrot, chopped

1 stalk celery, chopped

3 cloves garlic, minced

2 tsp. dried thyme

¼ cup wild rice

¼ cup barley

½ tsp. kosher salt

3 cups water

¼ cup brown rice

¼ cup cracked wheat

3 anchovy fillets

2 shallots, minced

1 TB. Dijon mustard

2 TB. red wine vinegar

2 large roma tomatoes, diced

1 large zucchini, grated

¼ cup fresh oregano, chopped

¼ cup fresh basil leaves, chopped

1 cup goat cheese, crumbled

Yield: 1 large salad
Prep time: 15 minutes
Cook time: 60 minutes
Serving size: ¼ salad

1. In a large sauté pan over high heat, heat 2 tablespoons olive oil. Add onion, carrot, celery, garlic, and thyme, and cook for 5 to 8 minutes or until tender.

2. Add wild rice and barley, and cook, stirring, for 5 to 10 minutes or until toasted and brown.

3. Add kosher salt and water, and bring to a boil. Reduce heat to low, cover, and cook for 15 minutes. At the 15-minute mark, stir in brown rice, and cook for 15 more minutes.

4. Add cracked wheat, and cook for 15 more minutes or until liquid is absorbed. Fluff with a fork, and spread onto a baking sheet to cool.

5. In a large bowl, whisk together anchovies, shallots, Dijon mustard, red wine vinegar, and remaining oil.

6. Add tomatoes, zucchini, and cooled grains. Toss to coat thoroughly, and chill for 30 to 60 minutes.

7. Mix in oregano, basil, and goat cheese just before serving.

 Salad Secret

Timing is the trick to this recipe because each grain requires a different cooking time. To make this recipe more manageable, get all your chopping and measuring done before you begin cooking.

Quinoa-Herb Salad

Herbs such as thyme, sage, and tarragon are the perfect complement to quinoa, adding interest and flavor but still letting the grain's nutty flavor shine.

4 cups water

1½ cups *quinoa*

1 large shallot, minced

¼ cup fresh thyme, minced

¼ cup fresh sage, minced

¼ cup fresh tarragon, minced

Zest and juice of 1 lemon

3 TB. olive oil

½ small red onion, diced

1 cup cherry tomatoes, halved

1 cucumber, diced

¼ cup fresh basil leaves

¼ cup fresh flat-leaf parsley leaves

½ cup sliced almonds

Yield: 1 large salad
Prep time: 40 minutes
Cook time: 20 minutes
Serving size: ¼ salad

1. In a large saucepan over high heat, bring water to a boil. Add quinoa, reduce heat to low, cover, and simmer for 15 minutes or until tender. Drain and spread onto a baking sheet to cool.

2. In a large bowl, mix together shallot, thyme, sage, tarragon, lemon zest, lemon juice, and olive oil.

3. Add onion, tomato, cucumber, and cooled quinoa. Stir thoroughly to coat, and chill at least 30 minutes.

4. Toss in basil, parsley, and almonds just before serving.

Lettuce Lingo

Quinoa is a tiny grain, first cultivated and cherished by the Incas and Aztecs. It's extremely high in protein and has a light, delicate flavor that pairs easily with all sorts of ingredients.

Chapter 11

Bean Salads

In This Chapter

- The benefits of beans
- Hearty and healthful classic bean salads
- Bean salads with international and exotic inspiration

Beans have been part of the human diet for centuries. The Ancient Egyptians knew them, as did the ancient cultures of the Americas.

Bean is a general term that encompasses several plants. It generally refers to the *legume*, large plant seeds found within long pods from plant family *fabaceae*. Soybeans, peas, lentils, and kidney beans are examples of legumes. When the seeds are dried, they're referred to as *pulses*. Many beans are only sold in dry form, while some, such as the pea, come both dried and fresh.

Beans are an excellent choice for low-fat protein, with more than twice the amount of protein as grain. They are a smart addition to any diet, but vegetarians, especially, use beans to achieve a daily source of complete protein.

Complete Protein

Protein is composed of 20 amino acids. Of the 20, 11 are called *nonessential* because our bodies make them, so we don't need to consume them. The remaining 9 amino acids are called *essential*, and it's important that you eat these every day.

Vegetarians, however, must seek out plant foods that contain proteins, consuming those with the right mixture of amino acids. It sounds complicated, but grains, nuts, and legumes each contain proteins not found in other plants, so adding a variety of these to the vegetarian diet does the trick.

Eating these plant foods in combination is called *complementary proteins*. When they're eaten over the course of a day, protein intake is complete. Protein derived from complementary plant proteins is considered a healthy alternative to meat, and by many people, a superior one. In addition to the protein, these combinations contain high-quality fiber, vitamins, minerals, and no saturated fat.

> **Tasty Morsel**
>
> Why worry about protein? Because you need it to build and maintain your muscles, organs, connective tissues, skin, bones, teeth, blood, and DNA (deoxyribonucleic acid). It helps your body heal when you're sick, wounded, and depleted.

Incorporating one of these bean-based salads in your weekly menu helps ensure your family stays deliciously healthy.

Canned Beans Versus Dried

Beans are available in dried or canned form. Canned beans are readily available, which makes it easy to add beans into your everyday diet.

Dried beans are less expensive, but they take longer to cook. They must first undergo a long soaking period to tenderize them. This is best done by covering them with cold water and letting them sit for 12 to 24 hours. Test a bean for moisture by cutting it in half. You'll be able to see how far the water has soaked into the bean. Once fully moistened, the beans are ready to be cooked. Cover them with clean cold water and simmer on low heat for 1 or 2 hours or until tender.

If you don't have time to soak beans, you can try the quick-soak method. Cover the beans with water, and bring to a boil over high heat. Remove from heat and let beans rest for 1 hour.

Tasty Morsel

Most beans contain *raffinose*, a type of sugar humans can't easily digest. Your small intestines complete the breakdown of most food, but your body lacks the enzymes needed to break down raffinose in the normal way. Consequently, this sugar is broken down in the large intestine by bacteria, which produces flatulence, or gas. Certain natural ingredients have been found to lessen this effect, as well as some man-made supplements. Spices such as caraway and dill, seaweed products, and the herb epazote, used in Latin cuisines, are often-used anti-gas ingredients.

Three-Bean Salad

This tangy, sweet recipe is a well-loved classic, standard at potlucks across the nation.

½ cup sugar

⅓ cup canola oil

½ cup tarragon vinegar

½ cup white wine vinegar

¼ tsp. kosher salt

¼ tsp. freshly ground black pepper

1 red, yellow, or green bell pepper, ribs and seeds removed, and chopped

1 (15-oz.) can kidney beans

1 (15-oz.) can yellow wax beans

1 (15-oz.) can green string beans

1 small red onion, chopped

2 scallions, chopped

| Yield: 1 large salad |
| Prep time: 45 minutes |
| Serving size: ¼ salad |

1. In a large bowl, whisk together sugar, canola oil, tarragon vinegar, white wine vinegar, kosher salt, and pepper.

2. Add bell pepper, kidney beans, yellow wax beans, green string beans, onion, and scallions. Toss well to coat, and chill for at least 30 minutes before serving.

 Salad Secret

This recipe is a great choice for outdoor parties because it contains no mayonnaise and can safely sit out in the sun all day. In fact, it tastes better when it's at room temperature.

Asian Bean Sprout Salad

The mixture of bean sprouts and soybeans is an interesting textural blend, and the bright flavor of the dressing adds the perfect touch.

2 cloves garlic, minced

1 TB. fresh ginger, grated

1 TB. sesame seeds

2 TB. sesame oil

1 TB. honey

¼ cup rice vinegar

3 scallions, chopped

4 cups *bean sprouts*

2 cups soybeans (edamame), shelled

1 cup fresh cilantro leaves

1 cup crunchy chow mien noodles

> **Yield: 1 large salad**
>
> **Prep time:** 45 minutes
>
> **Serving size:** ¼ salad

1. In a large bowl, combine garlic, ginger, sesame seeds, sesame oil, honey, and rice vinegar.

2. Add scallions, bean sprouts, and soybeans. Toss to thoroughly coat, and chill for at least 30 minutes.

3. Before serving, toss in cilantro leaves and chow mien noodles.

Lettuce Lingo

Bean sprouts are germinated beans. Mung bean sprouts are the most common, but others are available, including soybean and lentil sprouts. Seeds, like alfalfa and radish, produce smaller, threadlike sprouts.

Garbanzo-Bean and Roasted-Garlic Salad

Unlike its raw counterpart, roasted garlic is not strong and pungent, but mild and intensely sweet. It's the perfect accompaniment to the creamy garbanzo beans in this salad.

4 heads garlic

1 large eggplant

¼ cup olive oil

¼ tsp. kosher salt

¼ tsp. freshly ground black pepper

¼ cup *tahini*

Zest and juice of 1 lemon

2 TB. white wine vinegar

1 cucumber, diced

2 (15-oz.) cans garbanzo beans, drained and rinsed

¼ cup fresh flat leaf parsley, chopped

1 cup feta cheese, crumbled

2 or 3 cups pita chips

Yield: 1 large salad
Prep time: 45 minutes
Cook time: 30 minutes
Serving size: ¼ salad

1. Preheat the oven to 450°F.

2. Wrap garlic heads loosely in aluminum foil, and bake for about 30 minutes or until tender. Cool completely.

3. Meanwhile, dice eggplant, toss with 2 tablespoons olive oil, kosher salt, and pepper, and spread out onto baking sheet. Bake for about 15 minutes or until golden brown. Cool completely.

4. Cut cooled garlic in half cross-wise, and squeeze garlic paste into a large bowl. Add tahini, lemon zest, lemon juice, and white wine vinegar, and whisk thoroughly.

5. Add cucumber, cooled eggplant, and garbanzo beans, and stir together. Chill for at least 30 minutes.

6. Toss in parsley and feta, and serve with a handful of pita chips on the side.

Lettuce Lingo ⎯⎯⎯⎯⎯⎯⎯⎯⎯⎯⎯⎯⎯⎯⎯⎯⎯⎯⎯⎯⎯

Tahini is a smooth paste made from sesame seeds. It's a staple ingredient throughout the Middle East and is readily available in most large supermarkets.

Cuban Grilled Corn and Black Bean Salad

This Cuban-inspired salad takes full advantage of the smoky flavor of grilled corn.

4 ears sweet corn

3 TB. olive oil

3 cloves garlic, minced

1 small red onion, diced

Zest and juice of 2 large limes

Zest and juice of 1 orange

1 tsp. ground cumin

3 scallions, chopped

1 (4-oz.) can diced green chiles

1 small jicama, peeled and diced

2 large roma tomatoes

1 (15-oz.) can black beans, drained and rinsed

¼ cup fresh cilantro

1 cup ranchero cheese

Yield: 1 large salad
Prep time: 45 minutes
Cook time: 20 minutes
Serving size: ¼ salad

1. Preheat the grill to high.

2. Brush corn with 1 or 2 tablespoons olive oil, and grill briefly to mark on all sides. Cool.

3. In a large bowl, whisk together garlic, onion, lime zest, lime juice, orange zest, orange juice, cumin, and remaining olive oil.

4. Add scallions, green chiles, jicama, tomatoes, and black beans. Mix well, and chill for 30 to 60 minutes.

5. Using a large knife, carefully slice corn off cob. Add to beans, along with cilantro and ranchero cheese, toss to coat, and serve.

Tasty Morsel _____

Cuban culinarians use a mixture of herbs, onions, garlic, and chiles, called *sofrito*, to flavor sauces, meats, soups, and salads. This recipe uses a similar mixture of ingredients to impart a Cuban flavor.

Lentil Salad

The ingredients of this salad aren't exotic, but when combined with lentils and a cool vinaigrette, they certainly taste that way. Lightly spiced and a little tangy, it's a unique flavor experience.

1 cup dried lentils

2 bay leaves

1 tsp. dried thyme

2 cloves garlic, minced

1 TB. Dijon mustard

3 TB red wine vinegar

3 TB. olive oil

1 small white onion, chopped

2 stalks celery, chopped

1 large carrot, grated

1 cup ham, diced

Yield: 1 large salad
Prep time: 45 minutes
Cook time: 40 minutes
Serving size: ¼ salad

1. In a large saucepan, combine lentils, bay leaves, and thyme. Cover with water, and bring to a boil over high heat.

2. Reduce heat to low, and simmer, partially covered, for 30 minutes or until tender. Drain, discard bay leaves, and spread lentils on a baking sheet to cool completely.

3. In a large bowl, mix together garlic, Dijon mustard, red wine vinegar, and olive oil.

4. Add onion, celery, carrot, ham, and lentils. Toss to coat, and chill for at least 30 minutes before serving.

 Salad Secret

This dish can easily be made vegetarian by omitting the ham. And if you add 1 cup cooked rice or barley, it becomes a meal with complete protein.

String-Bean Salad

The prosciutto adds just a hint of saltiness to the bright, herby veggies in this crisp, fresh salad.

2 lb. fresh green beans, trimmed (about 7 cups)

1 lb. fresh yellow wax beans, trimmed (about 4 cups)

2 garlic cloves, minced

1 TB. fresh rosemary, minced or pulverized

Zest and juice of 1 lemon

¼ tsp. kosher salt

¼ tsp. freshly ground white pepper

1 small red onion, sliced

¼ lb. *prosciutto*, sliced thin

> **Yield: 1 large salad**
> **Prep time:** 45 minutes
> **Cook time:** 10 minutes
> **Serving size:** ¼ salad

1. Fill a large saucepan with water and bring to a boil over high heat. Add green beans and wax beans, and cook for 3 to 5 minutes or until their color brightens and they become slightly tender. Drain, submerge beans in ice water to cool, and drain again.

2. In a large bowl, mix together garlic, rosemary, lemon zest, lemon juice, kosher salt, pepper, onion, and prosciutto.

3. Add beans, toss to coat thoroughly, and chill for 30 to 60 minutes before serving.

Variation: Feel free to try this salad with frozen beans, or use a different green vegetable, like asparagus or broccoli.

Lettuce Lingo

Prosciutto means "ham" in Italian, but it generally refers to a salt-cured, air-dried, pressed ham from Parma. It's readily available in most large supermarkets, but any salty cured meat, like ham or salami, can successfully be substituted.

Tofu-Veggie Salad

Tofu absorbs flavors like a sponge, and the tangy garlic dressing on this salad is particularly suited to tofu's unique texture.

3 TB. olive oil

4 cloves garlic, minced

2 TB. cider vinegar

3 scallions, chopped

1 tsp. fresh dill, chopped

¼ tsp. kosher salt

1 (12- to 14-oz.) pkg. extra-firm *tofu*, pressed and crumbled

2 large roma tomatoes, diced

1 cup snow or snap peas, trimmed

1 cucumber, diced

¼ head purple cabbage, chopped (about 1 cup)

1 cup roasted peanuts, roughly chopped

Yield: 1 large salad
Prep time: 45 minutes
Cook time: 10 minutes
Serving size: ¼ salad

1. In a small sauté pan over medium heat, heat olive oil. Add garlic, and fry for 1 or 2 minutes or until golden. Immediately remove from heat, and pour into a large salad bowl.

2. Add cider vinegar, scallions, dill, and kosher salt, and whisk to combine. Add tofu, toss to coat, and chill for at least 30 minutes.

3. Before serving, add tomatoes, peas, cucumber, and cabbage. Toss thoroughly, and top with peanuts.

Lettuce Lingo

Tofu, also known as bean curd, is made from curdled soy milk in a process similar to that used to make cheese. Soybeans are rich in protein, so tofu is, too. It's also high in calcium and low in calories.

White Bean Salad

This Italian-inspired salad, full of garlic, herbs, and salty gorgonzola, pairs especially well with roasted meats like chicken or lamb.

2 cloves garlic, minced

3 TB. white wine vinegar

Zest and juice of 1 orange

¼ tsp. kosher salt

¼ tsp. freshly ground black pepper

¼ tsp. dried oregano

¼ tsp. dried sage

¼ tsp. fennel seeds, crushed

¼ cup olive oil

2 large roma tomatoes, diced

3 scallions, chopped

2 (15-oz.) cans cannellini beans, drained and rinsed

1 cup walnuts, toasted and chopped

1 cup *gorgonzola* cheese, crumbled

¼ cup fresh flat leaf parsley leaves

Yield: 1 large salad
Prep time: 45 minutes
Serving size: ¼ salad

Lettuce Lingo

Gorgonzola is an Italian blue cheese named for a town near Milan that was a center of dairy trade. The cheese is creamy and pungent and becomes stronger with age. Other blue cheeses may be substituted if necessary.

1. In a large bowl, whisk together garlic, white wine vinegar, orange zest, orange juice, salt, pepper, oregano, sage, fennel seeds, and olive oil.

2. Add tomatoes, scallions, and cannellini beans, toss thoroughly to coat, and chill for at least 30 minutes.

3. Before serving, toss in walnuts, gorgonzola cheese, and parsley. Serve with long croutons of toasted Italian garlic bread.

Chapter 12

Hearty Dinner Salads

In This Chapter

- Chopped and composed dinner salads
- Hearty salads with grilled and roasted meats
- Classic American and global favorite salads

There's no official definition of main dish or dinner salads, but most chefs agree that to qualify as a meal, a salad should contain a complete protein (see Chapter 11), a healthy amount of vegetables, and a grain source of some kind. Nonprofessionals may consider any salad that fills you up to be an adequate meal.

This chapter gives you a healthy sampling of salads that are a welcome substitute for standard dinner (or lunch) fare.

Peasant Food

In hard times, salads were a clever way to use leftovers. Small pieces of meat, cheese, a hard-boiled egg, and even day-old bread could be reinvented with the help of some fresh greens and a tangy dressing. Today, you just may pay a hefty price at your neighborhood bistro for similar concoctions.

Such frugal practices are still a great way to stretch your food budget. Try to plan ahead and grill an extra steak on barbecue night. Roast a bigger bird than you need, and save the leftovers. And don't be afraid to use meat from a can. Quality is good and, while the flavor may not be as great has home-roasted or grilled, once added to a spicy dressing the difference is negligible.

Save Time and Energy

Dinner salads can be quick and easy. And you can do lots in advance to save time when it counts.

Any salad elements that need to be cooked can easily be prepared in the morning, before the mercury rises, and spend the day in the fridge. You can rinse and chop vegetables early, too. Sturdy vegetables, like carrots, celery, radishes, cucumbers, and peppers can be stored in the fridge, chopped and submerged in water. Onions and garlic benefit from a soak in cold water, which leaches out the offensive oils that produce bad breath. Cheeses can be pre-grated, nuts pre-toasted, and dressings pre-mixed.

> **Salad Secret**
>
> Dinner salads can eliminate the need to turn on the oven. This factor is key on hot summer afternoons when everyone is hot and tired.

The only thing that doesn't benefit from pre-cutting is leaf lettuce. Chopping delicate leaves with a knife causes bruising and browning. This effect isn't usually noticeable, but if cut greens sit around for a while, the edges start to brown.

Taco Salad

Crunchy, spicy, creamy, and cool, this salad has it all. Best of all, it's easy, fast, and always a crowd pleaser.

2 TB. olive oil

3 cloves garlic, minced

1 large yellow onion, diced

1 lb. ground beef

2 tsp. ground cumin

2 or 3 tsp. chili powder

1 tsp. dried oregano

1 (15-oz.) can kidney beans, black beans, or pinto beans, drained and rinsed

1 cup sour cream

1 cup tomato salsa

½ head iceberg lettuce, shredded (about 2 cups)

1 large ripe tomato, chopped

1 cup grated cheddar cheese

3 scallions, chopped

1 (6-oz.) can sliced black olives

1 (4-oz.) can diced green chilies

4 cups tortilla chips

Yield: 1 large salad
Prep time: 15 minutes
Cook time: 15 minutes
Serving size: ¼ salad

1. In a large sauté pan over high heat, heat olive oil. Add garlic and onion, and cook for 2 or 3 minutes or until tender.

2. Add beef and cook for 3 to 5 minutes or until browned. Add cumin, chili powder, and oregano, and stir to combine. Remove from heat, drain off excess fat, and stir in beans.

3. In a small bowl, stir together sour cream and salsa.

4. In a large bowl, combine lettuce, tomato, cheese, scallions, olives, and green chilies. Add ground beef, beans, and salsa dressing.

5. Top salad with tortilla chips before serving.

Salad Secret

If you want to get fancy about it, you can omit the tortilla chips and serve the salad in a crispy tortilla bowl. Fry 1 large tortilla at a time in a deep pot of canola oil heated to 375°F. As it fries, press the tortilla in the middle with a large ladle to submerge it completely. Hold it in place for about 3 minutes or until it's golden brown. Remove with tongs, and drain on paper towels.

Cobb Salad

Be sure you get as many of this salad's fresh, crunchy, salty, ingredients to fit on each forkful as possible.

1 clove garlic, minced

1 tsp. sugar

¼ tsp. kosher salt

¼ tsp. freshly ground black pepper

1 TB. Dijon mustard

1 TB. Worcestershire sauce

1 TB. lemon juice

1 TB. red wine vinegar

3 TB. extra-virgin olive oil

4 cups mixed salad greens, washed and dried

2 cups cooked chicken meat, diced

1 ripe tomato, diced

2 hard-boiled eggs, peeled and chopped

6 slices bacon, cooked crisp and crumbled

1 ripe avocado, diced

1 cup Roquefort cheese, crumbled

Yield: 4 large salads
Prep time: 30 minutes
Serving size: 1 salad

1. In a large bowl, whisk together garlic, sugar, kosher salt, pepper, Dijon mustard, Worcestershire sauce, lemon juice, red wine vinegar, and olive oil.

2. Add salad greens, toss to coat, and divide evenly among 4 plates.

3. Arrange chopped chicken, tomato, eggs, bacon, avocado, and Roquefort cheese in sections on top lettuce. Serve chilled.

Tasty Morsel

This is style salad is commonly called a chopped salad. Each ingredient is cut to the same size, usually about ½- to ¾-inch dice

Southwestern Steak Salad

The smoky, charcoal flavor of grilled meat is the perfect match to spicy fresh chiles and fresh cilantro.

2 cloves garlic, minced

Zest and juice of 2 limes

¼ cup fresh cilantro, minced

½ tsp. kosher salt

½ tsp. freshly ground black pepper

½ cup olive oil

1½ lb. grilled flank steak, cooled and sliced thin against the grain

1 cup green onions, chopped

1 (15-oz.) can black beans, drained and rinsed

1 red bell pepper, ribs and seeds removed, and diced

1 large Anaheim chile, diced

1 large tomato, diced

Yield: 1 large salad
Prep time: 50 minutes
Serving size: ¼ salad

1. In a large bowl, whisk together garlic, lime zest, lime juice, cilantro, kosher salt, pepper, and olive oil.

2. Add steak, onions, black beans, red bell pepper, Anaheim chile, and tomato, and toss to coat.

3. Cover and chill for at least 30 minutes before serving.

Variation: This salad is a great way to use up leftover grilled meats. Feel free to get imaginative by using grilled chicken or fish instead of beef. Serve it with sour cream, guacamole, and a handful of tortilla chips.

> **Salad Secret** _____
>
> Flank steak is a thin, tough cut of beef. Served like a normal steak, it would be too tough to eat. But slicing thin against the grain breaks through the fibers and makes it easier to eat. Such cuts can also benefit from extended marinating in an acid-based mixture, which naturally softens the protein fibers.

Chicken Fajita Salad

The picante spices, lime, and cilantro make this a south-of-the-border version of a classic chicken salad.

½ cup sour cream

2 TB. Dijon mustard

2 cloves garlic, minced

Zest and juice of 2 small limes

1 tsp. ground cumin

½ tsp. dried thyme

½ tsp. dried oregano

¼ tsp. cayenne

¼ tsp. freshly ground white pepper

3 scallions, chopped

1 red bell pepper, ribs and seeds removed, and sliced

1 small red onion, sliced

2 large roma tomatoes, diced

4 cups cooked chicken meat, diced

¼ cup fresh cilantro leaves

2 cups romaine lettuce, shredded

| **Yield: 4 large salads** |
| **Prep time:** 40 minutes |
| **Serving size:** 1 salad |

1. In a large bowl, whisk together sour cream, Dijon mustard, garlic, lime zest, lime juice, cumin, thyme, oregano, cayenne, and white pepper.

2. Add scallions, red bell pepper, onion, tomatoes, and chicken. Toss thoroughly to coat, and chill for at least 30 minutes.

3. In a large bowl, combine cilantro leaves and shredded romaine, and divide evenly among 4 serving plates. Top each plate with chilled chicken salad.

Variation: For a little something more, serve this salad with tortilla chips or warm flour tortillas.

Tasty Morsel _____

The fajita is a Texas original, probably started by Mexican Vaqueros working Texas cattle round-ups.

Chinese Chicken Salad

The crunch in this popular salad comes from several ingredients, including fried rice noodles.

1 or 2 cups peanut oil

2 cups *rice noodles,* fried

2 TB. sesame oil

Zest and juice of 1 lemon

2 TB. rice vinegar

2 TB. honey

¼ cup soy sauce

2 cups cooked chicken, diced or shredded

2 cups romaine lettuce, shredded

2 cups napa cabbage, shredded

2 medium carrots, peeled and sliced thin on an angle

2 scallions, sliced thin on an angle

1 (8-oz.) can sliced water chestnuts, drained

¼ cup cashews, chopped

Yield: 1 large salad
Prep time: 50 minutes
Cook time: 20 minutes
Serving size: ¼ salad

1. In a heavy skillet over high heat, heat 1 inch of peanut oil to 375°F. Test oil with a small piece of noodle. If it sizzles immediately, it's ready. Add noodles in batches, and fry for less than 30 seconds or until puffed and crisp. Drain on paper towels.

2. In a large bowl, whisk together sesame oil, lemon zest, lemon juice, rice vinegar, honey, and soy sauce.

3. Add chicken, lettuce, cabbage, carrots, scallions, and water chestnuts. Toss thoroughly to coat, and chill for at least 30 minutes.

4. Just before serving, toss in rice noodles and cashews.

Rice noodles, or rice stick or cellophane noodles, look like thin threads of plastic or fishing line. When fried, they puff up into airy, crunchy noodles.

Italian Bread Salad

This salad is known as Panzanella in Italian, and it's the ultimate peasant food, made to utilize stale bread. The bread soaks up the fresh flavors of the vegetables and dressing in a heartier version of the standard crouton.

2 cloves garlic, minced

Zest and juice of 1 lemon

3 TB. balsamic vinegar

1 tsp. fennel seed, crushed

1 tsp. dried oregano

¼ cup olive oil

1 small red onion, sliced thin

1 red bell pepper, ribs and seeds removed, and sliced thin

4 large roma tomatoes, diced

1 large cucumber, diced

1 fennel bulb, sliced thin

1 large loaf Italian bread, diced into 1-in. cubes

1 cup fresh basil leaves, chopped

Yield: 1 large salad
Prep time: 90 minutes
Serving size: ¼ salad

1. In a large bowl, stir together garlic, lemon zest, lemon juice, balsamic vinegar, fennel seed, oregano, and olive oil.

2. Add onion, red bell pepper, tomatoes, cucumber, and fennel. Toss together to coat thoroughly.

3. In a separate bowl, alternately layer bread and vegetable salad in 4 layers. Cover with plastic wrap, and chill for 1 hour.

4. Before serving, toss well, adding basil at the last minute.

Salad Secret

Stale bread is preferable in this recipe, because it's lost its moisture and is, therefore, more accepting of the flavorful dressing. If you can plan ahead, cube your bread 8 to 24 hours in advance, and let it sit out at room temperature.

Middle Eastern Cucumber, Pita, and Bean Salad

Fresh and cool, this salad is a perfect accompaniment to spicy, flavorful kebabs and curries.

1 cup nonfat plain yogurt

1 tsp. ground cumin

2 TB. chopped fresh mint

$\frac{1}{2}$ tsp. kosher salt

4 medium cucumbers, peeled, seeded, and sliced

1 medium red onion, sliced

1 (15-oz.) can garbanzo beans, drained and rinsed

4 cups pita chips

Yield: 1 large salad

Prep time: 90 minutes

Serving size: ¼ salad

1. In a large bowl, mix together yogurt, cumin, mint, and salt.

2. Add cucumbers, onion, and garbanzo beans. Cover with plastic wrap, and refrigerate for 1 hour.

3. Just before serving, toss in pita chips.

Salad Secret

If you have the opportunity to buy English cucumbers, do so. They have fewer seeds and cause fewer burps.

Glossary

al dente   Italian for "against the teeth." Refers to pasta, rice, or vegetables that are neither soft nor hard, but just slightly firm against the teeth.

allspice   Named for its flavor echoes of several spices (cinnamon, cloves, nutmeg), allspice is used in many desserts and in rich marinades and stews.

almonds   Mild, sweet, and crunchy nuts that combine nicely with creamy and sweet food items.

anchovies (also **sardines**)   Tiny, flavorful preserved fish that typically come in cans. Anchovies are a traditional garnish for Caesar salad, the dressing of which contains anchovy paste.

anise   An annual flowering herb related to parsley. The seeds have a distinctive licorice flavor, which is used in liqueurs, candies, sauces, and cosmetics.

antioxidants   Molecules that slow oxidation of other molecules. Oxidation can produce free radicals, which trigger chain reactions that damage cells. In addition to preventing these reactions, antioxidants can inhibit them, once begun.

antipasto   A classic Italian-style appetizer, usually served together as one course or plate, including an assortment of prepared meats, cheeses, and vegetables such as prosciutto, capicolla, mozzarella, mushrooms, and olives.

artichoke hearts   The center part of the artichoke flower, often found canned in grocery stores.

arugula   A spicy-peppery garden plant with leaves that resemble a dandelion and have a distinctive—and very sharp—flavor.

baguette   A long, narrow loaf of crisp, crusted white French bread with a light, chewy interior.

bake   To cook in a dry oven. Dry-heat cooking often results in a crisping of the exterior of the food being cooked. Moist-heat cooking, through methods such as steaming, poaching, etc., brings a much different, moist quality to the food.

balsamic vinegar   Vinegar produced primarily in Italy from the trebbiano grape and aged in wood barrels for as many as 25 years. It is heavier, darker, and sweeter than most vinegars.

barbecue   To quick-cook over high heat, or to cook something long and slow in a rich liquid (barbecue sauce).

basil   A flavorful, almost sweet, resinous herb delicious with tomatoes and used in all kinds of Italian or Mediterranean-style dishes.

beat   To quickly mix substances.

black pepper   A biting and pungent seasoning, freshly ground pepper is a must for many dishes and adds an extra level of flavor and taste.

blanch   To place a food in boiling water for about 1 minute (or less) to partially cook the exterior and then submerge in or rinse with cool water to halt the cooking. Also referred to as *parboiling*.

blend   To completely mix something, usually with a blender or food processor, more slowly than beating.

blue cheese   A blue-veined cheese that crumbles easily and has a somewhat soft texture, usually sold in a block. The color is from a flavorful, edible mold that is often added or injected into the cheese.

boil   To heat a liquid to a point where water is forced to turn into steam, causing the liquid to bubble. To boil something is to insert it into boiling water. A rapid boil is when a lot of bubbles form on the surface of the liquid.

bok choy (also **Chinese cabbage**) A member of the cabbage family with thick stems, crisp texture, and fresh flavor. It's perfect for stir-frying.

brine A highly salted, often seasoned, liquid used to flavor and preserve foods. To brine a food is to soak, or preserve, it by submerging it in brine. The salt in the brine penetrates the fibers of the meat and makes it moist and tender.

broil To cook in a dry oven under the overhead high-heat element.

brown rice Whole-grain rice including the germ with a characteristic pale brown or tan color; more nutritious and flavorful than white rice.

brown To cook in a skillet, turning, until the food's surface is seared and brown in color, to lock in the juices.

bulgur A wheat kernel that's been steamed, dried, and crushed and is sold in fine and coarse textures.

capers Flavorful buds of a Mediterranean plant, ranging in size from is *nonpareil* (about the size of a small pea) to larger, grape-size caper berries produced in Spain, pickled in salty, vinegar-based brine.

caramelize To cook sugar over low heat until it develops a sweet caramel flavor. The term is increasingly gaining use to describe cooking vegetables (especially onions) or meat in butter or oil over low heat until they soften, sweeten, and develop a caramel color.

caraway A distinctive spicy seed used for bread, pork, cheese, and cabbage dishes. It is known to reduce stomach upset, which is why it is often paired with, for example, sauerkraut.

cardamom An intense, sweet-smelling spice, common to Indian cooking, used in baking and coffee.

cayenne A fiery spice made from (hot) chile peppers, especially the cayenne chile, a slender, red, and very hot pepper.

celery root The edible, bulbous root of the celery plant. Also known as celeriac.

cheddar The ubiquitous hard cow's milk cheese with a rich, buttery flavor that ranges from mellow to sharp. Originally produced in England, cheddar is now produced worldwide.

cheesecloth   A fine linen mesh cloth, traditionally used in cheese making to strain whey from curds. Also used to strain foods as well as cover, wrap, or steep them.

chili paste   Toasted, re-hydrated, and puréed dried chiles.

chili powder   A seasoning blend that includes chile pepper, cumin, garlic, and oregano. Proportions vary among different versions, but they all offer a warm, rich flavor.

chili sauce   A condiment similar to ketchup, made with chiles, chili powder, tomatoes, and vinegar.

chile   Any one of many different "hot" peppers, ranging in intensity from the relatively mild ancho pepper to the blisteringly hot habanero.

chives   A member of the onion family, chives grow in bunches of long leaves that resemble tall grass or the green tops of onions and offer a light onion flavor.

chop   To cut into pieces, usually qualified by an adverb such as "*coarsely* chopped," or by a size measurement such as "chopped into $^1/_2$-inch pieces." "Finely chopped" is much closer to mince.

cider vinegar   Vinegar produced from apple cider, popular in North America.

cilantro   A member of the parsley family and used in Mexican cooking (especially salsa) and some Asian dishes. Use in moderation, as the flavor can overwhelm. The seed of the cilantro is the spice coriander.

cinnamon   A sweet, rich, aromatic spice commonly used in baking or desserts. Cinnamon can also be used for delicious and interesting entrées.

clove   A sweet, strong, almost wintergreen-flavor spice used in baking and with meats such as ham.

coriander   A rich, warm, spicy seed used in all types of recipes, from African to South American, from entrées to desserts.

count   In terms of seafood or other foods that come in small sizes, the number of that item that compose 1 pound. For example, 31- to 40-count shrimp are large appetizer shrimp often served with cocktail sauce; 51- to 60-count are much smaller.

couscous Granular semolina (durum wheat) that is cooked and used in many Mediterranean and North African dishes.

croutons Chunks of bread, usually between $1/4$ and $1/2$ inch in size, sometimes seasoned and baked, broiled, or fried to a crisp texture and used in soups and salads.

cumin A fiery, smoky-tasting spice popular in Middle-Eastern and Indian dishes. Cumin is a seed; ground cumin seed is the most common form used in cooking.

curing A method of preserving uncooked foods, usually meats or fish, by either salting and smoking or pickling.

currants Tiny raisins made from miniature zante grapes. Don't confuse them with red, white, or black currants, which are small berries used for preserves, pastries, and the liqueur cassis.

curry Rich, spicy, Indian-style sauces and the dishes prepared with them. A curry uses curry powder as its base seasoning.

curry powder A ground blend of rich and flavorful spices used as a basis for curry and many other Indian-influenced dishes. Common ingredients include hot pepper, nutmeg, cumin, cinnamon, pepper, and turmeric. Some curry can also be found in paste form.

daikon A large Asian radish, with white flesh and white, red, or black skin. Daikon can grow up to 1 foot long and as much as 4 inches in diameter.

dash A few drops, usually of a liquid, released by a quick shake of, for example, a bottle of hot sauce.

devein The removal of the dark vein from the back of a large shrimp with a sharp knife.

dice To cut into small cubes about $1/4$-inch square.

Dijon mustard Hearty, spicy mustard made in the style of the Dijon region of France.

dill A herb perfect for eggs, salmon, cheese dishes, and, of course, vegetables (pickles!).

dollop A spoonful of something creamy and thick, like sour cream or whipped cream.

drizzle To lightly sprinkle drops of a liquid over food, often as the finishing touch to a dish.

dry In the context of wine, a wine that contains little or no residual sugar, so it's not very sweet.

emulsion A combination of liquid ingredients that do not normally mix well, beaten together to create a thick liquid, such as a fat or oil with water. Creation of an emulsion must be done carefully and rapidly to ensure that particles of one ingredient are suspended in the other.

entrée The main dish in a meal. In France, however, the entrée is considered the first course.

extra-virgin olive oil *See* olive oil.

fennel In seed form, a fragrant, licorice-tasting herb. The bulbs have a much milder flavor and a celerylike crunch and are used as a vegetable in salads or cooked recipes.

feta A white, crumbly, sharp, and salty cheese popular in Greek cooking and on salads. Traditional feta is usually made with sheep's milk, but feta-style cheese can be made from sheep's, cow's, or goat's milk.

fillet A piece of meat or seafood with the bones removed.

fish sauce A liquid condiment and ingredient similar in appearance to soy sauce made from fermented fish.

flake To break into thin sections, as with fish.

floret The flower or bud end of broccoli or cauliflower.

fold To combine a dense and light mixture with a circular action from the middle of the bowl.

frittata A skillet-cooked mixture of eggs and other ingredients that's not stirred but is cooked slowly and then either flipped or finished under the broiler.

fry *See* sauté.

fuji A crisp, sweet Japanese apple.

garbanzo beans (or **chickpeas**) A yellow-gold, roundish bean used as the base ingredient in hummus, garbanzo beans are high in fiber and low in fat.

garlic A member of the onion family, a pungent and flavorful element in many savory dishes. A garlic bulb contains multiple cloves. Each clove, when chopped, provides about 1 teaspoon garlic. Most recipes call for cloves or chopped garlic by the teaspoon.

ginger Available in fresh root or dried, ground form, ginger adds a pungent, sweet, and spicy quality to a dish.

Gorgonzola Commonly referred to as a blue-vein cheese, Gorgonzola is an Italian cow's milk cheese that has veins that appear more green than blue. Gorgonzola can be creamy, crumbly, or firm. Its piquant flavor comes from the addition of bacteria, added and allowed to germinate into mold.

grate To shave into tiny pieces using a sharp rasp or grater.

grind To reduce a large, hard substance, often a seasoning such as peppercorns, to the consistency of sand.

Gruyère A rich, sharp cow's milk cheese made in Switzerland that has a nutty flavor.

handful An unscientific measurement; the amount of an ingredient you can hold in your hand.

haricot vert Small, thin French green beans.

Havarti A creamy, Danish, mild cow's milk cheese perhaps most enjoyed in its herbed versions such as Havarti with dill.

hazelnuts (also **filberts**) A sweet nut popular in desserts and, to a lesser degree, in savory dishes.

hearts of palm Firm, elongated, off-white cylinders from the inside of a palm tree stem tip.

herba salata Latin for "salted herbs," this is the origin of the word *salad*.

herbes de Provence A seasoning mix including basil, fennel, lavender, marjoram, rosemary, sage, savory, and thyme, common in the south of France.

hoisin sauce A sweet Asian condiment similar to ketchup, made with soybeans, sesame, chili peppers, and sugar.

hors d'oeuvre   French for "outside of work" (the "work" being the main meal), an hors d'oeuvre can be any dish served as a starter before the meal.

horseradish   A sharp, spicy root that forms the flavor base in many condiments from cocktail sauce to sharp mustards. Prepared horseradish contains vinegar and oil, among other ingredients. Use pure horseradish much more sparingly than the prepared version, or try cutting it with sour cream.

hummus   A thick, Middle Eastern spread made of puréed garbanzo beans, lemon juice, olive oil, garlic, and often tahini (sesame seed paste).

ice bath   Ice water used to quickly cool foods. Foods can be placed in directly or set on top in another bowl and stirred until cool.

infusion   A liquid in which flavorful ingredients such as herbs have been soaked or steeped to extract that flavor into the liquid.

Italian seasoning   A blend of dried herbs and spices, including basil, fennel, oregano, rosemary, and thyme.

jicama   A juicy, crunchy, sweet, large, round Central American vegetable. If you can't find jicama, try substituting sliced water chestnuts.

julienne   A French word meaning "to slice into very thin pieces," julienne-cut foods are cut into long, thick, matchstick-size pieces.

kalamata olives   Traditionally from Greece, these medium-small long black olives have a smoky rich flavor, a result of being marinated in wine and olive oil.

Key limes   Very small limes grown primarily in Florida known for their tart taste.

kosher salt   A coarse-grained salt made without any additives or iodine.

legume   A plant species that contains seeds inside a long pod. In culinary language, *legume* refers to the fresh seed from inside the pod.

lentils   Tiny lens-shape pulses used in European, Middle Eastern, and Indian cuisines.

macerate   To soak food, usually fruit, in liquid to infuse flavor.

marinate To soak meat, seafood, or other food in a seasoned sauce, called a marinade, which is high in acid content. The acids break down the muscle of the meat, making it tender and adding flavor.

marjoram A sweet herb, a cousin of and similar to oregano, popular in Greek, Spanish, and Italian dishes.

mascarpone An Italian triple cream cheese, soft like clotted or sour cream, and mild in flavor.

meld To allow flavors to blend and spread over time. Melding is often why recipes call for overnight refrigeration and is also why some dishes taste better as leftovers.

mesclun Mixed salad greens, usually containing lettuce and assorted greens such as arugula, cress, endive, and others.

microplane A fine grater used for citrus zest and hard cheeses. The tool was originally a carpenter's rasp used for sanding wood.

mince To cut into very small pieces smaller than diced pieces, about $1/8$ inch or smaller.

mold A decorative, shaped metal pan in which contents, such as mousse or gelatin, set up and take the shape of the pan.

niçoise olives Olives similar in flavor and appearance to black kalamata olives but much smaller.

nutmeg A sweet, fragrant, musky spice used primarily in baking.

Old Bay A spice blend from Chesapeake Bay used to season seafood. It consists of celery seeds, bay, mustard, cinnamon, and ginger.

olive oil A fragrant liquid produced by crushing or pressing olives. Extra-virgin olive oil—the most flavorful and highest quality—is produced from the first pressing of a batch of olives; oil is also produced from later pressings.

olives The fruit of the olive tree commonly grown on all sides of the Mediterranean. Black olives are also called ripe olives. Green olives are immature, although they are also widely eaten. *See also* kalmata olives.

oregano A fragrant, slightly astringent herb used in Greek, Spanish, and Italian dishes.

orzo   A rice-shape pasta used in Greek cooking.

oxidation   The browning of fruit flesh that happens over time and with exposure to air. Minimize oxidation by rubbing the cut surfaces with a lemon half. Oxidation also affects wine, which is why the taste changes over time after a bottle is opened.

paprika   A rich, red, warm, earthy spice that also lends a rich red color to many dishes.

parboil   To partially cook in boiling water or broth, similar to blanching (although blanched foods are quickly cooled with cold water).

parchment paper   Heavy paper that withstands heat, water, and grease used to line pans and wrap foods.

Parmesan   A hard, dry, flavorful cheese primarily used grated or shredded as a seasoning for Italian-style dishes.

Parmigiano-Reggiano   A hard grating cheese named for the area of its origin—Parma, Italy. It's considered the best, but fine-quality Parmesan is also made in other countries, including the United States.

parsley   A fresh-tasting green leafy herb, often used as a garnish.

pecans   Rich, buttery nuts, native to North America, that have a high unsaturated fat content.

peppercorns   Large, round, dried berries ground to produce pepper.

pesto   A thick spread or sauce made with fresh basil leaves, garlic, olive oil, pine nuts, and Parmesan cheese. Some newer versions are made with other herbs.

pickle   A food, usually a vegetable such as a cucumber, that's been pickled in brine.

pilaf   A rice dish in which the rice is browned in butter or oil and then cooked in a flavorful liquid such as a broth, often with the addition of meats or vegetables. The rice absorbs the broth, resulting in a savory dish.

pinch   An unscientific measurement term, the amount of an ingredient—typically a dry, granular substance such as an herb or seasoning—you can hold between your finger and thumb.

pine nuts (also **pignoli** or **piñon**)   Nuts grown on pine trees, that are rich (read: high fat), flavorful, and a bit pine-y. Pine nuts are a traditional component of pesto and add a wonderful hearty crunch to many other recipes.

pink peppercorns   Unrelated to white and black peppercorns, these dried berries come from ornamental trees native to Brazil.

pita bread   A flat, hollow wheat bread often used for sandwiches or sliced, pizza style, into slices. Terrific soft with dips or baked or broiled as a vehicle for other ingredients.

poach   To cook a food in simmering liquid, such as water, wine, or broth.

porcini mushrooms   Rich and flavorful mushrooms used in rice and Italian-style dishes.

portobello mushrooms   A mature and larger form of the smaller crimini mushroom, portobellos are brownish, chewy, and flavorful. Often served as whole caps, grilled, and as thin sautéed slices. *See also* crimini mushrooms.

preheat   To turn on an oven, broiler, or other cooking appliance in advance of cooking so the temperature will be at the desired level when the assembled dish is ready for cooking.

prosciutto   Dry, salt-cured ham, that originated in Italy.

pulse   The dried seed from a legume.

purée   To reduce a food to a thick, creamy texture, usually using a blender or food processor.

quinoa   An ancient Incan grain, and one of the few vegetable sources of complete protein.

rancid   Oxidation of oil that results in foul flavor and odor.

reduce   To boil or simmer a broth or sauce to remove some of the water content, resulting in more concentrated flavor and color.

render   To cook a meat to the point where its fat melts and can be removed.

reserve   To hold a specified ingredient for another use later in the recipe.

rice vinegar   Vinegar produced from fermented rice or rice wine, popular in Asian-style dishes. Different from rice wine vinegar.

ricotta   A fresh Italian cheese smoother than cottage cheese with a slightly sweet flavor.

Roquefort   A world-famous (French) creamy but sharp sheep's-milk cheese containing blue lines of mold.

rosemary   A pungent, sweet herb used with chicken, pork, fish, and especially lamb. A little of it goes a long way.

rotini   An Italian pasta shaped like a corkscrew.

sage   An herb with a musty yet fruity, lemon-rind scent and "sunny" flavor.

salsa   A style of mixing fresh vegetables and/or fresh fruit in a coarse chop. Salsa can be spicy or not, fruit-based or not, and served as a starter on its own (with chips, for example) or as a companion to a main course.

sauté   To cook food quickly, over high heat, constantly stirring for even browning.

savory   A popular herb with a fresh, woody taste.

Scoville scale   A scale used to measure the "hot" in hot peppers. The lower the Scoville units, the more mild the pepper. Mildly hot ancho peppers are about 3,000 Scovilles; Tears of Fire and habanero peppers are 30,000 Scovilles or more.

sear   To quickly brown the exterior of a food, especially meat, over high heat to preserve interior moisture.

sesame oil   An oil made from pressing sesame seeds, that's tasteless if clear and aromatic and flavorful if brown.

shallot   A member of the onion family that grows in a bulb somewhat like garlic and has a milder onion flavor. When a recipe calls for shallot, use the entire bulb.

shellfish   A broad range of seafood, including clams, mussels, oysters, crabs, shrimp, and lobster. Some people are allergic to shellfish, so take care with its inclusion in recipes.

sherry A fortified wine from the Andalusian region of southern Spain. There are several varieties, ranging from dry Manzanillas to sweet Olorosos.

shiitake mushrooms Large, dark brown mushrooms with a hearty, meaty flavor. Can be used either fresh or dried, grilled or as a component in other recipes and as a flavoring source for broth.

short-grain rice A starchy rice popular for Asian-style dishes because it readily clumps (perfect for eating with chopsticks).

shred To cut into many long, thin slices.

simmer To boil gently so the liquid barely bubbles.

skillet (also **frying pan**) A generally heavy, flat-bottomed metal pan with a handle designed to cook food over heat on a stovetop or campfire.

skim To remove fat or other material from the top of liquid.

slice To cut into thin pieces.

star anise A potent anise-flavored spice from a star-shape fruit from an evergreen tree.

steam To suspend a food over boiling water and allow the heat of the steam (water vapor) to cook the food. A quick cooking method, steaming preserves the flavor and texture of a food.

steep To let sit in hot water, as in steeping tea in hot water for 10 minutes.

Stilton The famous English blue-veined cheese, delicious with toasted nuts and renowned for its pairing with Port wine.

stir-fry To cook small pieces of food in a wok or skillet over high heat, moving and turning the food quickly to cook all sides.

stone fruit A tree fruit that contains a pit, or stone, such as peaches apricots, cherries, and plums.

sweet anise Another name for fennel, though the actual herb anise is unrelated.

tahini A paste made from sesame seeds used to flavor many Middle Eastern recipes.

tarragon   A sweet, rich-smelling herb perfect with seafood, vegetables (especially asparagus), chicken, and pork.

thyme   A minty, zesty herb.

toast   To heat something, usually bread, so it's browned and crisp.

tofu   A cheeselike substance made from soybeans and soy milk.

trebbiano   A grape used extensively in the production of white wine.

turmeric   A spicy, pungent yellow root used in many dishes, especially Indian cuisine, for color and flavor. Turmeric is the source of the yellow color in many prepared mustards.

twist   A garnish for an appetizer or other dish, usually made from a lemon or other citrus fruit. To make, cut a thin, $1/8$-inch-thick cross-section slice of a lemon or other fruit. Cut from the center of that slice out to the edge on one side. Pull apart the two cut ends in opposite directions.

tzatziki   A Greek appetizer and sauce containing yogurt, mint, dill, and garlic.

vegetable steamer   An insert for a large saucepan or a special pot with tiny holes in the bottom designed to fit on another pot to hold food to be steamed above boiling water. *See also* steam.

venison   Deer meat.

vinegar   An acidic liquid widely used as dressing and seasoning, often made from fermented grapes, apples, or rice. *See also* balsamic vinegar; cider vinegar; rice vinegar; white vinegar; wine vinegar.

walnuts   A rich, slightly woody flavored nut.

wasabi   Japanese horseradish, a fiery, pungent condiment used with many Japanese-style dishes. Most often sold as a powder; add water to create a paste.

water bath   A method in which a pan of food is cooked resting in another, larger pan of water. The method slows the conduction of heat, cooking slowly and gently. The method is known in French as a *bain marie*.

water chestnuts   A tuber, popular in many types of Asian-style cooking. The flesh is white, crunchy, and juicy, and the vegetable holds its texture whether cool or hot.

whisk   To rapidly mix, introducing air to the mixture.

white mushrooms   Button mushrooms. When fresh, they have an earthy smell and an appealing "soft crunch."

white vinegar   The most common type of vinegar, produced from grain.

whole-wheat flour   Wheat flour that contains the entire grain.

wild rice   Actually a grass with a rich, nutty flavor, popular as an unusual and nutritious side dish.

wine vinegar   Vinegar produced from red or white wine.

Worcestershire sauce   Originally developed in India and containing tamarind, this spicy sauce is used as a seasoning for many meats and other dishes.

yeast   A tiny fungi that, when mixed with water, sugar, flour, and heat, release carbon dioxide bubbles, which causes the bread to rise.

zest   Small slivers of the colorful, outermost rind of a citrus fruit, usually lemon, lime, or orange. Zest contains the potent citrus oils that give the fruit its flavor.

zester   A kitchen tool used to scrape zest off a fruit. A small grater also works well.

Index

W-X-Y-Z

The *fun* cookbook library

Fondues
& Hot D...

978-1-59257-...

Smoothies

978-1-59257-318-9

Snac...
Cak...

978-1-5925...

Sushi &
Sashimi

978-1-59257-782-8

Chec...   ...ing titles

ALPHA
idiotsguides.com